P.B. WAITE is Professor Emeritus of History at Dalhousie University. Among his earlier books are *John A. Macdonald: His Life and World* and *The Man from Halifax: Sir John Thompson, Prime Minister*.

Canada's bachelor prime ministers have always provided extraordinary material for biographers. Richard Bedford Bennett is no exception. In this volume P.B. Waite offers three entertaining essays on the personal life of Canada's Depression prime minister.

The first essay is set in New Brunswick, where Bennett grew up. It focuses on Bennett's youth and the early influences on his character: school, church, and family. The second, covering his years as a Calgary businessman and an Ottawa MP, explores the development of Bennett's political ideas, his views on the British Empire and Canada's place within it. The third essay covers his years as Conservative leader and prime minister; it deals with the women in Bennett's life, particularly his close relationship with his sister and his romance with Hazel Kemp Colville.

After his death in 1947, Bennett's devoted secretary destroyed many of his personal papers. Waite has risen masterfully to this challenge. In his skilful hands the private Bennett is revealed in a new and fascinating light.

THE LONER

Three Sketches
of the Personal
Life and Ideas
of R.B. Bennett
1870–1947

The 1991 Joanne Goodman Lectures

P.B. WAITE

University of Toronto Press
Toronto London Buffalo

© University of Toronto Press Incorporated 1992
Toronto Buffalo London
Printed in Canada

ISBN 0-8020-2894-2 (cloth)
ISBN 0-8020-7401-4 (paper)

Printed on acid-free paper

Canadian Cataloguing in Publication Data

Waite, P.B. (Peter Busby), 1922–
The loner

(The 1991 Joanne Goodman lectures)
Includes index.
ISBN 0-8020-2894-2 (bound) ISBN 0-8020-7401-4 (pbk.)

1. Bennett, R.B. (Richard Bedford), 1870-1947.
2. Bennett, R.B. (Richard Bedford), 1870-1947 —
Personality. 3. Prime ministers — Canada —
Biography. 4. Politicians — Alberta — Biography.
I. Title. II. Series: The Joanne Goodman
lectures ; 1991.

FC576.B46W34 1992   971.062'3'092   C92-094392-6
F1033.B46W34 1992

The Joanne Goodman Lecture Series

has been established by Joanne's family

and friends to perpetuate the memory of her

blithe spirit, her quest for knowledge, and

the rewarding years she spent at the

University of Western Ontario.

Contents

Foreword

The Joanne Goodman Lectures were established at the University of Western Ontario in 1975 to honour the memory of the elder daughter of Mr and Mrs Edwin Goodman of Toronto. Each year the university invites a scholar to deliver the three lectures on some aspect of the history of the English-speaking peoples, particularly those of the Atlantic Triangle of Canada, the United Kingdom, and the United States, that will be of interest to members of the university community and the general public. The list of those who have so far participated in the series indicates the distinction of these lectures and the part they play in the intellectual life of the institution. The University of Western Ontario is grateful to Mr Goodman and his family and friends for this generous and moving benefaction dedicated to a student who loved history and enjoyed her years at this university.

Although Peter Waite is indelibly identified with Dalhousie University, where he has been a faculty member for over forty years, latterly as Thomas McCulloch Professor until his retirement in 1988, he has made a practice of being a visiting professor every twenty-five years in the Department of History at the University of Western Ontario, where we also regard him with admiration and affection as a distinguished and congenial colleague, sentiments which are extended to include Masha. On the second occasion in our midst, in 1988–9, he held the J.B. Smallman chair in history. As one of Canada's leading historians, and an exceptionally elegant stylist, he has held many other lectureships and visiting lectureships elsewhere. He is a Fellow of the Royal Society of Canada, a former president of the Canadian Historical Association, and the recipient of honorary degrees from several universities.

We at Western were particularly delighted when Peter Waite agreed to interrupt his usual cycle of visits to deliver these lectures and share with us his view of the shape of R.B. Bennett's life, 'the figure under the carpet' that will inform his more extensive work on Bennett's career after 1927. The Bennett who emerges is a far more sympathetic and humane person than hitherto generally supposed, concerned with social problems from his Methodist youth, very attractive to others, but above all, as Arthur Meighen observed, 'a man of deep feelings and deep affections.' Through the generosity of the lecture trust this discussion can now be shared by a wider audience as an introduction and anticipation of the biography that Bennett's lifelong friend, Lord Beaverbrook, tried for years to get a scholar of Peter Waite's standing to write.

Neville Thompson
The University of Western Ontario

Preface

Joanne Goodman was a second-year history student at the University of Western Ontario when she died as the result of a highway accident in April 1975. Her parents commemorated her elegantly with a yearly series of lectures. It is a great honour to have been asked to give the 1991 Goodman Lectures, and to join the select group of historians who have preceded me. Mr Edwin Goodman and my colleagues at the University of Western Ontario have been most gracious; their hospitality bade fair to undermine whatever equanimity the 1991 lecturer may have brought with him from Nova Scotia.

I have to thank the Social Science and Humanities Research Council of Canada for funding research on R.B. Bennett, and James Gray of Calgary, with whom for several years I have shared ideas and discoveries about Bennett, surely one of the more neglected of our twentieth-century prime ministers. I am especially grateful to Professor Carman Miller and his wife, Pamela, of McGill University, who told me about R.B. Bennett's 1932 letters to Hazel Colville, and to Mrs Colville's daughter, Mrs Frances Ballantyne, who kindly invited me to lunch and talked about her mother and her mother's famous caller.

Mary Wyman typed the manuscript with a celerity I have come

to rely on, and Diane Mew has done much to transform three lectures into printable prose; I have almost invariably followed her pertinent advice.

P.B.W.
Halifax, Nova Scotia
March 1992

Introduction

R.B. Bennett enjoys, probably, the worst reputation of any Canadian prime minister. Chubby Powers's 1932 jibe, made in the House of Commons, that in Bennett's public relations he 'often exhibits the manners of a Chicago policeman, and the temperament of a Hollywood actor,' made headlines in Canadian newspapers. It had just enough truth in it to make it stick.[1]

Bennett is full of contradictions. Alice Millar, his personal secretary for thirty years, remarked in 1957 to Lord Beaverbrook, when they were still looking for a biographer, 'I cannot understand how anyone can bring R.B. Bennett alive, with all his character and colour, without having known him.'[2] She didn't help. She was an enthusiastic laundress. She went through R.B. Bennett's papers telling R.B.'s brother, Ronald V. Bennett, 'I keep those [papers] that have historic value and tear up the rest.'[3] Professor A.G. Bailey recalls walking through the woods behind the University of New Brunswick one windy day and finding a letter of Beaverbrook's to Bennett in among the trees. It had blown from the incinerator; Alice Millar was destroying 'unhistorical' letters in the Bennett Papers. Bailey gathered up whatever he could find.[4] Beaverbrook had a good sense of history; he did not like destroying anything, and he began to wonder if the Bennett Papers would yield up enough of personal interest to make Bennett a believable figure. In the end, Beaverbrook wrote his own biography of Bennett out of his own collection of Bennett Papers.[5]

R.B. Bennett did not help much either. He himself destroyed his letters to his mother, his letters to and from Mrs Eddy, and no doubt others; he has to be sought out in other sources besides his own papers, although some of those will bear another searching look, particularly the few letters extant from his sister Mildred.

It is not the purpose of these lectures to give another biography of R.B. Bennett. Biographies exist. They may be useful, or feeble, or represent a struggle of the biographer against a fate too overwhelming, such as Ernest Watkins's biography of 1963. My purpose is to try to explain the personal side of R.B.'s life, his character, his ideas, and, where I can, what went into the making of both. His political career will be only peripheral; I have taken R.B. himself as centre, and left the rest for the time being. James Gray has recently published a book on Bennett's Calgary years, and eventually I may attempt the subsequent one. These three lectures are a series of discrete sketches, across three main periods of Bennett's life, aiming to suggest different elements of that complex, vibrant personality.

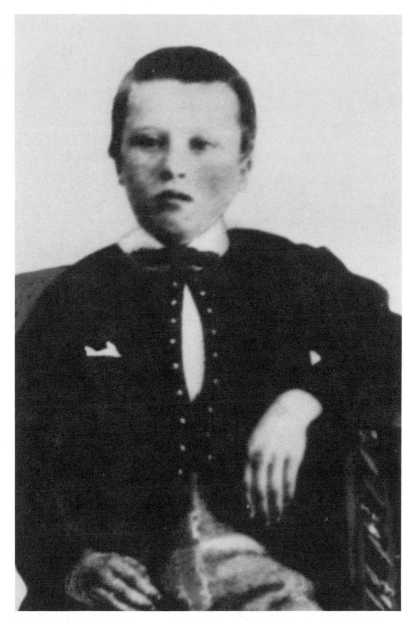

Dick Bennett aged about ten, at Hopewell Cape, New Brunswick

As a young lawyer in Chatham, New Brunswick, *c.* 1894

Bennett in 1912: the Calgary corporation lawyer and rising politician

Bennett and his sister Mildred at his swearing in as prime minister,
7 August 1930

'My Government.' A Bennett
cabinet, as interpreted by
Arch Dale of the Winnipeg
Free Press in 1931

Mrs Hazel Colville, the widow who came into Bennett's life in 1932, pictured here in a studio portrait of 1924

Bennett after his heart trouble in 1935, a weary but still determined prime minister

Bennett walking in his sixty-acre country estate, Juniper Hill, Surrey, 1943

The elderly Viscount Bennett: a portrait taken in 1945, two years before his death

1 〜

Hopewell Cape and the Miramichi 1870-1897

RICHARD BEDFORD BENNETT was born at Hopewell Hill, where the little Shepody River comes down to Chignecto Bay; he was raised at Hopewell Cape, eight miles away, where the mighty Petitcodiac does the same.[1] Between these two, he spent most of the first sixteen years of his life.

Chignecto Bay is a huge funnel narrowing towards the northeast as it approaches the Petitcodiac. Hopewell Cape is where the two can be said to meet. At each new moon the tides at Hopewell Cape run at forty-seven feet between low water and high. The result is dramatic: most of the water in every little harbour goes out to sea twice a day, and twice a day comes flooding back again. These mighty tides are forced into a narrowing funnel. At Moncton, fifteen miles up river, the tide arrives as a wall of water nearly four feet high. Three hours before full high tide, one can hear it coming.

The Petitcodiac and its Shepody Bay have turbid water, laden with sediment, red-brown, like the soil of the land. What is shore, shoal, sand, sea is difficult to distinguish. A large tidal river separates the lands it drains, for those great tides are to be watched and feared; the river is thus vacillating, inscrutable, dangerous. People that lived along the river had two kinds of time, sun time and tide time. The ferry that crossed the Petitcodiac at Hopewell Cape could only run by tide time.[2]

Like Westmorland County across the river, Albert County was, and is, a countryside of dykes and distances, the forests behind the river and sea being tribute to the shore. Charles G.D. Roberts grew up across the river in the village of Westcock, not ten miles from Hopewell Cape, living there from 1860 to 1874. Like R.B. Bennett, its world was stamped into his being. He remembered 'an unremitting wind, blowing down the vast and solitary and green levels of Tantramar, bowed all one way the deep June grasses over the miles on miles of marsh ... The scene was all space – all high, light colour, wind-washed brightness, and loneliness.'[3]

The other end of the year, when the great winter storms came winding up Chignecto Bay past Cape Enrage, was not without loneliness either. Those snow-laden gales could bury fences, roads, and all man-made things. In 1882, when R.B. Bennett was eleven years old, there was a succession of storms, the mail getting through in only five days out of fourteen. The snow was so deep it was difficult even to get the cattle to water. A farmer not far away recorded in his diary for Sunday, 26 February 1882:

A three-day snowstorm, wind north-east, no passing for four days. Roads all blocked up with snow ... A cruel storm ... Business generally suspended. Cannot drive or get around, roads so bad. As soon as they are broken out and become passable at all, another storm comes and fills them in again. Snow over the tops of fences most everywhere, and in some places three or four feet higher than the fences. Apple trees cannot be seen, only the tops of them ...[4]

In June, though, the apple trees look very different, and the countryside glows with grass and new leaves and blossoms. There is good land here, and under the hot sun it looks both fruitful and placid. The heat that often besets inland New Brunswick in the summer is mercifully cut in the afternoon by the southwest breeze from the sea. Indeed, in May and June that breeze can bring on sudden and blinding fogs, rolling in from the Bay of Fundy, cutting off the sun, and chilling everything within its grasp. That Bay of Fundy poet Bliss Carman described it:

Those tall navies of disaster,
The pale squadrons of the fog,
That maraud this gray world border
Without pilot, chart, or log
Ranging wanton as marooners
From Minudie to Manan.[5]

That is when the foghorn down at Cape Enrage begins to sound its own litany of loneliness, like a weird seawolf, out on the twin heads.

Albert County was carved out of Westmorland County in 1845 and in 1871 it had a population of 10,672. Of the labour force, 75 per cent were farmers, 10 per cent sailors, and most of the rest shipbuilders and carpenters. Some 5 per cent mined gypsum and albertite, the jet-black bituminous mineral named after the county in which it was found. Sawmills were everywhere, but by the 1870s dairying, with butter and cheese-making, was gaining ground over more traditional occupations.[6]

Hopewell Cape was a shipbuilding village in mid-century, making the vessels that took gypsum and plaster to Maine or Boston, lumber to Saint John. In the 1871 census its population was over eighteen hundred. At least two hundred vessels were built along the Petitcodiac between 1825 and 1903: schooners, brigs, brigantines, barques, even full-rigged ships. Some were built for the captains that sailed them; some were 'company' ships with several men in shares; others were built for firms farther down the Bay of Fundy. The great Bay of Fundy schooner trade would be in place for many a year yet. The little ports around the rim of the bay were still tied to the empire of Saint John: St Martin's, Dorchester, Maccan, Parrsboro, Maitland, all the way down to Digby, Brier Island, and Grand Manan. There would be schooners at the Market Slip in Saint John to the end of the 1930s, and after. Bliss Carman described one:

There's a schooner out from Kingsport,
Through the morning's dazzle-gleam,
Snoring down the Bay of Fundy
With a norther on her beam.[7]

In the 1870s the railway came, building down from west of

Moncton; it rejoiced in the title of the Salisbury, Hillsborough and Albert Railway. It was a great boon to many, for it promised easy transportation to the Intercolonial Railway at Moncton, and complemented Hopewell Cape's designation in 1875 as the county seat of Albert County. The railway did not augur so well for shipping; the Bennett shipyard at the cape, originally well-equipped, found the new railway, and competition, hard going.

The Bennetts were old Yankee stock, not United Empire Loyalists, who had come to Nova Scotia in 1761. The family had come out from England in 1635 and settled in southwestern Massachusetts, which became Connecticut by the end of the seventeenth century. They had settled at Lyme, near the mouth of the Connecticut River. By the 1760s, with the Appalachians, the Indians, and British policy blocking off expansion westward, there was a substantial New England migration eastward and northward, into the lands the British had newly taken from the French. In Nova Scotia that started in the 1760s, before the Seven Years' War was over, fishermen going to the south shore to found fishing towns such as Mahone Bay, Chester, Bridgewater, and farmers going to the Annapolis valley to the fat lands vacated by the Acadians. Zadok Bennett, aged twenty-eight, with his wife Mary and three children, left Lyme in 1761, and took up five hundred acres of land near present-day Wolfville, in the usual New England pattern, with a town lot in the village of Horton. They subsequently migrated across the Bay of Fundy to the Petitcodiac, where by the 1840s R.B. Bennett's grandfather, Nathan Bennett, had established a solid reputation as a shipbuilder.[8]

He had started his own shipyard with a younger brother in 1848. They did well. Their biggest vessel was the *Favorite*, a ship-rigged three-master of eight hundred tons, built mostly of hackmatack. Nathan's son Henry, after an education at Mount Allison Academy, joined the firm in 1860 as clerk. By 1868 he had become a partner in his father's business. A year later he married Henrietta

Stiles, a school teacher at Hopewell Hill, eight miles to the west of Hopewell Cape.

Neither the shipyard nor the marriage went all that well. Business began falling off in the 1870s, and Henry Bennett had to turn himself into a general merchant and farmer. Suspicion was that he drank, and that he lacked the will to run a new profession. The best he could do was eventually to become a justice of the peace for Albert County. R.B. Bennett rarely talked about his father. One source, accurate in most respects, declared that Bennett was 'the son of a hard-drinking blacksmith and a teetotal school teacher,' a juxtaposition sufficiently striking.[9] Certainly, Henry Bennett's Baptist persuasion did not necessarily mean that he was an abstainer. From whatever cause, his livelihood contracted; to feed his growing family (there were four children born between 1870 and 1876) he had to make shift somehow. He went through money easily, in spite of the all too palpable necessity to save it.[10]

The family's great tower of strength was Henrietta Stiles Bennett. The Stiles, like the Bennetts, were old Yankee stock. She was a Methodist, and came from a modestly prosperous seafaring family at Hopewell Hill. Her faith was made of strong stuff, and her eldest son became the vessel that carried all her hopes and values for the future, in the absence of any very substantial present. As for R.B., or Dick as everyone called him, his mother was, as he once put it, the very 'main spring' of his life. It was his joy and ambition to please her. As a child he would listen to her reciting Longfellow, then Tennyson, and later, Byron and Milton. She taught him history, of 'the empires of old' as he put it, and of that great modern empire, the British; and especially, she taught him 'the beauties of higher mathematics.' She was everything to her eldest son, 'teacher, guide, counsellor, companion, friend and above all an impartial and candid critic.'[11]

She had been born on 13 July 1844. She had a bright mind

and auburn hair – and a temperament to go with them. Both were inherited by her eldest son, born nine and a half months after her marriage. Young Dick Bennett early gave evidence of characteristics that he would retain for a long time: a temper, quick and easy assimilation of knowledge, and an aptitude for mathematics and history. Hopewell Cape also had a remarkable teacher who would glorify history by having his students act it. Mary Queen of Scots was executed in Bennett's very classroom. Dick had a turn for drama; and he was an excellent mimic. He was also good at debating. But he was a solitary soul. Occasionally his mother would encourage him to have a party at home; he would ask certain boys, each of whom would in turn ask a girl and bring a pound of sugar; Mrs Bennett would make candy with the sugar. Still, he was not really popular with the other lads. They could not understand his dedication to diligence, his supreme commitment to honesty, in fact to his mother's values. He did not play hookey or steal apples. His integrity gave him a faint miasma of tale-bearing.[12] This, with his studious bent, made him solitary, aloof, perhaps even a 'mother's boy,' a label that makes every normal twelve-year-old cringe. He was big enough and strong enough to be able to take care of himself; that and his temper meant he was not to be trifled with.

His mother was a Wesleyan Methodist, but in the 1871 census R.B. Bennett, aged one, was set down as a Baptist. That may have been because there was then no Methodist church in Hopewell Cape; the local population there was largely Baptist. Altogether, Albert County was 60 per cent Baptist, 20 per cent Methodist. In the 1881 census, after the establishment of the Hopewell Cape Methodist Church, all the children and their mother were set down as Wesleyan Methodist.[13]

By birth and training Wesleyan, Henrietta Stiles had many of the characteristics of the breed: a natural aversion to ostentation; a deep commitment to the ethic of work – sloth to her was, as it was to Wesley, a sin. Indulgence was bad stewardship of oneself.

Labour was itself a virtue; it was not a punishment for sin, nor a grim necessity dictated by Genesis 3.19, 'by the sweat of thy face shalt thou eat bread.' Thrift, industry, honesty, sobriety, generosity, were the pre-eminent Christian virtues in Methodist households such as the one in which R.B. Bennett grew up.

Peculiar to the Methodist creed was its view of money. Money was not evil: love of money was. Like any commodity, money could be used well or badly. Wesley would say, Earn all you can, lawfully by honest industry, hurting not your neighbours, and selling goods and services at a fair price:

Gain all you can by honest industry: use all possible diligence in your calling. Lose no time ... Every business will afford some employment sufficient for every day and every hour ... [and] will leave you no leisure for silly unprofitable diversions. You have always something better to do ... Do it as soon as possible. No delay! No putting off from day to day or from hour to hour ... And do it as well as possible. Do not sleep or yawn over it. Put your whole strength to the work. Spare no pains. Let nothing be done by halves ... Let nothing in your business be left undone if it can be done by labour and patience.[14]

Then, having by honesty and unwearied diligence worked hard, Wesley's second rule followed: 'Save all you can.' Do not throw away that precious talent on gratifying mere desires of the flesh. 'Despise delicacy and novelty, and be content with what plain nature requires.' Forget expensive furniture, costly pictures, or elegant (as opposed to useful) gardens. The purpose was not to accumulate a fortune for yourself or your children. Having first earned all you could, then saved as much as you could, then, said Wesley, give all you can. And do not stint yourself in the process.[15]

In this context Methodism was neither revolutionary nor reactionary; it was, rather, bourgeois. It was ascetic, in one important sense of that tradition. In North America this turned a little solemn perhaps,[16] not always joyful, but fearless, strong and, especially, tolerant. 'We think and let think,' as Wesley once put it.[17] Man's wickedness was not owing to bad environment or poor education, but was simply inherent in the human animal. John Wesley's mother insisted that wilfulness was the main cause of sin in the world, and sought to eradicate it in her own children. In short, the life Methodism inculcated was modest, austere, responsible, sober, hard-working, and honest; conservative socially; it was charitable to the world, exacting to the inner self.

Wesley sought a disciplined and responsible Christian life; every Christian must be a steward, of himself, of his family, of others. He sought not only a religion of personal salvation, of personal hope and confidence in redemption, but a religion that embodied duties to society. Wesley's view of holiness was a social holiness as much as a personal one. This double theme is well illustrated in his sermon 'The Good Steward,' whose stewardship comprehended looking after the 'reasonable wants' of oneself and one's family, after which the rest was to go to society, 'feeding the hungry, clothing the naked, comforting the sick, assisting the stranger, relieving the afflicted.'[18] Bennett would later quote Disraeli to the same effect: 'Look further, look further yet, which is there to remedy and redeem!'[19]

What, specifically, of all of this, Henrietta Stiles Bennett conveyed to her eldest son, in the absence of any letters from her, it is impossible to know. But Bennett's devotion in later years is surely the reflection of lessons learned early and long from his school-teacher mother. Charity was one great virtue he practised. His mother also constantly whetted his ambition, made more necessitous by the failing financial health of the Bennett family. Aim high, she would say, aim at the stars. As for work, she got him to memorize part of Longfellow's 'Ladder of St Augustine':

The heights by great men reached and kept
Were not attained by sudden flight,

But they, while their companions slept,
Were toiling upward in the night.[20]

One can recognize John Wesley's words and injunctions in many of Bennett's actions, then and later. He allowed more for luck, chance, and a leg up from friends when one needed it. But Bennett's fundamental morality was that Methodist inheritance, delivered to him in that most potent form – from a mother whom he admired and adored, whose mind was at once a source of knowledge and guide to his springs of action.

Allowance should be made also for the effects upon the son who, from birth, had been the focus on his mother's passionate adoration and her unrealized hopes from her marriage. Henrietta Bennett found in her tall, good-looking eldest son the fulfilment of her own ambitions, which had been frustrated by her easygoing, gregarious husband. Such husbands can make a vigorous and intelligent woman very unhappy; charming no doubt when young, captivating even, such men do not always wear well in the long run. Their talents as sportsmen, or good companions, do not measure up so readily to the hard exigencies of the market. Bennett's father was never able to carve out a niche for himself and his family, either in the world he knew or in any other. Henry Bennett exhausted capital, he did not create it; his fortunes thinned as the 1870s drew on, and his family began to live a life close to the bone. His drinking, which his wife hated, did not help. In that respect she certainly bent her son to her passionate belief that drinking was the root of most evil.

Whether all of this made young Bennett neurotic is a question; Freudians could make much of it. Was he indeed subject, any more than most people, to strong unconscious conflicts between felt instincts and perceived duties? Ernest Watkins in *R.B. Bennett* finds this neurosis, and makes it the main explanation of Bennett's 'furious energy, his driving ambition, his inability to work with others on terms of equality ... his outbursts of temper, his apparent arrogance and insensitivity to those around him.'[21] This may be so; but most mothers love their sons, the eldest ones not least, and one hesitates before the simplicity of Watkins's explanations. Bennett loved his mother all his life; one need not accept an explanation that stems from Freud's overheated Viennese sexuality.

Certain it is, however, that at the age of sixteen, in 1886, young Bennett had to face making his own way in the world. He had learned by now to count every penny. There had been no question of his going into his father's business; there was really none to go into. But he was a natural teacher, quick to learn, and apt at imparting what he learnt. He could interest an audience in what he had to say. Turning to school-teaching required only a licence obtained by a three-month stint at normal school. In the autumn of 1886 he went to the normal school in Fredericton and obtained a second-class licence. That allowed him to teach junior grades. In that group there were 180 student teachers, forty men and 140 women; and most of them were very young, sixteen to eighteen on average.[22]

Almost immediately Dick Bennett got a teaching post at a country school at Irishtown, near Moncton, for which he was paid $160 per annum. The new teacher's possessions were in a little black trunk, mostly books. Bennett's main interests were biography, poetry, and the Bible. His favourite poets were Longfellow and Whittier, those New England poets whose images, principles, and hopes spoke straight to Maritimers.

School was taught, so he reported, for twenty-four weeks and five Saturdays, January to June of 1887.[23] He did the fall term of 1887, then went again to Fredericton in January 1888, for the six months necessary to get his first-class licence. He was in the top third of his class for marks, and the bottom third for deportment. Almost as soon as he was finished, the trustees at Douglastown, up on the Miramichi, appointed him principal of their school. In that lumbering community, perhaps the lower grade for deportment would be an advantage.

The Miramichi was half a day's train journey to the north of Hopewell Cape on the Intercolonial, the railway crossing the river at Newcastle on the way north to the Baie des Chaleurs. The southwest Miramichi rises just fifteen miles east of New Brunswick's border with Maine and the rich potato fields of the Saint John valley. It ends in the Gulf of St Lawrence, 150 miles or more to the northeast. Three branches of it meet just above Newcastle and flow eastward another twenty-five miles to strike the sea in Miramichi Bay. The river at this point is almost three-quarters of a mile wide. Its sheer size dictated the creation of two lumber towns, Newcastle on the north shore, Chatham on the south, the latter five miles downstream. The two towns are quite different. Newcastle is pitched on the side of a hill; the roads run down on an angle into the town, and the cross-streets run parallel to the river, block by block in easy stages, rising above it. There is nothing as steep as the brutality of the hills in old Saint John; at Newcastle the hill is high enough for contemplation of the valley, and not so steep that one has to work for it.

Chatham, down river, has a simpler time with its geography. Water, Duke, and Wellington streets run parallel to the river; in summer the frame houses wear their age, like their trees, with a quiet dignity, unlike the raucous world that had given the town birth half a century before. There is lots of time in Chatham; the river's current is real, but it is unhurried, like life itself there. Chatham produced the Cunards and other families, and the cemetery of the 1823 Anglican Church holds their bones.

The predominant architecture of both towns, and of Douglastown, in 1888 as now, is what architects call Second Empire – the houses with gambrel roofs and high windows to let the light into the high second storeys. The manse built at Newcastle in 1882 for the Reverend William Aitken, the father of the redoubt-

able Max, is a characteristic and spacious example. The Presbyterians were, indeed, the main religion of the Miramichi, and
William Aitken's church, St James and St John, crowns the hill
even now, with its white spire and colonial nave.

Douglastown is three miles downriver from Newcastle, on the
same north side. That is where Dick Bennett arrived in October
1888. The school trustees had hired a principal who had just
turned eighteen, without interview, on the basis on his record
and his recommendations out of Fredericton. When he came he
looked even younger than he was. Alma Russell, daughter of the
Douglastown postmaster, witnessed his arrival in the village that
early October day; she thought him a most unpromising looking
specimen: tall (six feet), slim, freckled, sitting bolt upright on the
wagon seat, underneath a bowler hat too large for him.[24] He
supervised the operations of four little schools, with three lady
teachers and 159 students. He himself taught the upper grades,
six, seven, and eight. He established a reputation of being able,
firm, and fair. He liked students to memorize poetry, not so much
as academic exercise, but to give them lines to reflect about, that,
as he put it,

would come to us in our dull moments, to refresh us as with spring
flowers; in our self musings, to win us by pure delight from the
tyranny of foolish castle building, self congratulations and mean
anxieties. They may be with us in the work-shop ... on pleasant hill-
sides or by sounding shores – noble friends and companions – our
own! Never intrusive, ever at hand, coming at our call.

He had a penchant for wanting contemporary information, illustrated by his grade eight geography examination for 1889, which
asked his students what and where were: Esquimalt, Digby, Pe-
terborough, Mistassini, Stanstead. This question illustrated the
catholicity of his own information, and was not easy. His 1889
spelling examination was also demanding: it included words such

as immeasurably, analogies, prerogatives, disembarkation, sequestered, haranguing, penuriously. And if his examinations were hard, they were marked in the same way.[25]

Nevertheless, his punishments were mild; probably his temper and his moral authority did good service, and he did not need a heavy hand. Some older girls were punished by making them sit on the long bench that went around the walls of the room. Another Bennett punishment was to have the pupil stand at the window with his slate and write a composition on what was passing by on the Douglastown road.[26] He was as tough on parents and trustees as on the students. He told the parents that unless they aroused themselves from their apathy, the fine potential of their children would never be realized. As for the trustees, he did not spare them either. 'I would remark,' he noted in his year-end report of June 1890 to the Board of School Trustees, District No. 6, Newcastle, 'that the school officials are sadly deficient in their duties. During my [two-year] stay here I have not been favoured by a visit from one of the trustees.'[27]

He had by that time established a local reputation for quick repartee, ready speech, and rhetoric. Alma Russell remembered a jingle from Fredericton Normal School days:

First there came Bennett conceited and young
Who never knew quite when to hold his quick tongue.

Alma did not believe that. She thought young Bennett knew what he could do and he was forthright enough to say so.[28]

Dick Bennett was fond of girls, but he was shy, sentimental, and vulnerable. When he was growing up, dancing was not common, and neither he nor his brother Ronald learned to dance. Mildred and George, the younger siblings, did. As the eldest, Dick seems not to have had much opportunity to collect social skills. Not only that, but as school teacher, especially as principal, he had to behave with considerable circumspection. But much of his asceticism came from within, taken straight from John Wesley's Methodism via his mother, and with his father as a living example of how the human animal could sometimes go awry. His morality comprehended no smoking, no cards, no drinking, and, as it turned out, no dancing.

There was some irony in this, for the Miramichi village and town debating and literary clubs, where he might have excelled, were gradually giving way to outdoor sports. In winter this meant skating, curling, tobogganing, and before long, hockey. In none of this was Dick Bennett very skilled or very interested. Thus, his life in Douglastown was not without its loneliness. Picnics on the Miramichi were a happy summer and fall diversion; the steamer would leave Newcastle in the morning, stop at Douglastown, go on to Chatham on the south bank, then a few miles farther on to the sea beaches. It was a day's expedition, and the picnickers would return in the evening, sometimes by moonlight. On the way down, one fine day in 1889 a slender young man in a light suit and a straw hat was leaning on one of the piers at Douglastown as the steamer stopped. A lady asked her friend, 'Isn't that young man coming too?' 'Oh, no,' said her friend, 'he's a teacher here.' Still, the lady thought the teacher would have liked to have come, if he'd been asked.[29]

But young school principals, even the conscientious and socially uncertain ones, learn the ways of the world of the Miramichi. Dick Bennett must not be thought of as a stick, devoid of any sense of fun or adventure. At one picnic, in the summer of 1889 or 1890, just for the amusement of the group he was with, he went into a field where a white horse was grazing. He caught it and mounted, using a newspaper for saddle. The horse was greatly astonished, and careered around the field with Dick successfully aboard. The rider eventually got off without injury to himself or the horse, but the newspaper was a mess! The group were riveted by the performance.[30]

The friendship between Dick Bennett and Max Aitken began in the spring of 1889. The relationship was not without its ups and downs, but they appealed to each other even then, across the nine years that separated their ages. Max was impish, mischievous, and fun-loving. Bennett was more sober-sided, with the impishness in his eyes and wit. Their differences were also religious. Max was Presbyterian, and he liked to tease Dick with a poem Bennett hated:

I know that God is wrath with me
For I was born in sin.
My heart is so exceeding vile
Damnation dwells therein.
Awake I sin, asleep I sin,
I sin with every breath.
When Adam fell he went to hell
And damned us all to death.[31]

Whenever Beaverbrook was ill he thought he could hear the flames of hell roaring for him. There was no such agonizing in Bennett's Christianity. Methodism was a religion of hope, not despair. Bennett's confidence and Max's desperation (when he was ill) was one obvious measure of the difference between Methodists and Presbyterians. Part of Bennett's delight in Max was his sheer irrepressibleness. Bennett never minded being talked back to; he liked a bit of steel on steel. As he gathered confidence, he also liked to scare people and admired them if they weren't intimidated.

A friend recalled a picnic a year or two later with Dick Bennett, Max Aitken, Jimmy Dunn, and one or two others, including a visitor from Ottawa. Max and a friend, Harold Girvan, gathered firewood along the beach, while Dick sat on the sand keeping the others in roars of laughter as they got supper ready over the fire. Bennett was always a brilliant conversationalist, Girvan remembered. Jimmy Dunn, on the other hand, sat quietly, digging information out of the visitor from Ottawa.[32]

By January 1890, Dick Bennett had made the acquaintance of Lemuel Tweedie, a lawyer in Chatham, and MLA for Northumberland. He began to work Saturdays there, first helping Tweedie in the provincial election of February 1890, and then helping out with office work. Sometimes he would cross the frozen Miramichi on snowshoes. In April Tweedie asked Bennett to stay on, working Saturdays until school ended and for the summer months after that. Tweedie's offer obviously comprehended an apprenticeship in law. Undecided at first whether to abandon a teaching career already started, Dick closed with the offer in mid-May. By then he was considering law school, McGill or Dalhousie. He had saved enough, perhaps half his teaching income, to be able to manage at least the first year. Fees at Dalhousie were $40 a year, and room and board in Halifax about $18 a month. Altogether a university year would cost him around $150.[33]

Thus it was that in the fall of 1890, at the age of twenty, Dick Bennett, instead of returning across the river to the principal's job at Douglastown school, took train at Newcastle for Hopewell Cape and Halifax. He spent a day at the Cape seeing his family, helping with the haying; then on 5 September he went across the Petitcodiac on the ferry, got the Intercolonial at Dorchester, and arrived in Halifax.

Halifax is generally described in the early Baedeker of Canada (mine is the 1907 edition) as 'beautifully situated ... enclosed by its splendid harbour.' Dick Bennett liked it at once. Within twenty-four hours he had rooms in a boarding-house on South Street, two or three blocks from Dalhousie. By Monday he was enrolled under the already famous Dean Richard Weldon, and was soon into 'talk, walk and work' as he put it, well pleased with what he was doing.[34]

He made a decided impression in the law school's mock parliament, which everyone went to, including the dean. The *Dalhousie Gazette* noted him, in November of 1890, bristling with facts in debate. 'He will be a good one yet ...' By the next year he was called Sir Ricardo Brindle-Back Bennett, champion in the lists, striking fear into the untried ranks of the term's new government. He missed his Miramichi friends, but found political excitement in the visit of Sir John A. Macdonald, Sir John Thompson, and Sir Charles Tupper who celebrated with Conservative friends at a large picnic on 1 October. Dick Bennett was proud to shake hands with 'our good old man,' the prime minister. It was Sir John's fence-mending expedition, providential as it turned out, for the federal election of 5 March 1891 was brought on very suddenly. It summoned both the dean of law and one of his students, Dick Bennett.[35]

Weldon was unusual in believing that a lawyer not only had a responsibility to his practice, his work, and his clients, but also that he had a duty to public service.[36] Weldon himself exemplified that spirit of sacrifice in being elected as MP for Albert County, New Brunswick, in the 1887 election. The Dalhousie Law School term was in consequence peculiar; it began two weeks before the regular arts and science classes, but it ended early in February, two months before the others. That allowed the dean of law to go to Ottawa for the session of the House of Commons! With young Bennett helping his 1891 canvass, Weldon was re-elected in 1891. Bennett loved it all. He clipped the satirical anti-Liberal poem in the Halifax *Evening Mail* in that very anti-American election, 'Sir Richard Cartwright's Lament':

We're not ready for the fight, Jimmy Blaine;
Old Tomorrow's got us tight, Jimmy Blaine;
He has jumped upon us hard,
He has trumped our strongest card

He has played low down, old pard, Jimmy Blaine.

If we'd had another year, Jimmy Blaine;
(Pray excuse this silent tear), Jimmy Blaine;
Old Tomorrow made a scoop,
And his Party's cock-a-hoop
And your friends are in the soup, Jimmy Blaine.[37]

The Dalhousie Law School being geared to the sessions of Parliament, by late March 1891 Dick Bennett was already back in Tweedie's office in Chatham. There he got the news that he had passed his examinations, and so well that he was surprised. His first-year record was the best of any of his years. In Crimes and in Contracts he was first in a class of twenty-four; in Constitutional History and in Real Property he was second.[38] He was even better than he thought.

His unrelenting, driving ambition left him little time for anything but that which served it. His fellow students at Dalhousie never saw him at a rugby game; his interests centred on the library, the Moot Court, the Mock Parliament. He had outstanding ability and as those examination results had come in, he was more than ever aware of it. When he returned to Dalhousie from the Miramichi in the autumn of 1891, he could not resist preening himself on his academic prowess. That did not sit well at Dalhousie, where one was supposed to carry one's triumphs with some modesty. His fellows were not having any of that New Brunswick boastfulness. They ganged up on him, not physically but academically. They divided classes between them, each student concentrating on one subject, resolved that Bennett would not get better than second place in any class. This worked only partly in 1891–2, for Dick Bennett still took first place in two subjects; but in his last year, 1892–3, he was no better than third in any subject. This plot had the unexpected side effect of forcing

the conspirators to work hard, and they did much better themselves than they would have otherwise![39]

In his first year at Dalhousie, Dick had had letters from the
Miramichi that suggested any romance with Alma Russell might
be at an end. One letter, he said in his diary, had destroyed 'the
last relic of the days long ago [!] when I was so foolish to run
around with a girl called A.[lma] R.[ussell]. Vanitas vanitas omnia
est vanitas.' Despite that, during the summer of 1891, working
happily in the law office of Tweedie, he would row across the
mile or so of pretty water to visit with the Russell family.[40]

Whatever the result of Dick Bennett's flirtation with Alma Russell, it is a fact that in 1892 she decided to move west to Victoria
to join her family. Dick drove the buggy that took her and her
belongings to the Newcastle station; they were not to meet again
for several years. Alma married a Fred Yorston, but there was
either a death or possibly a divorce, for she eventually resumed
her maiden name. All Bennett's extant letters to her, from 1914
to 1946, suggest an old and treasured acquaintance that had be-
gun in happy days on the Miramichi.[41]

The autumn of 1892 marked Dick Bennett's most expansive
term at Dalhousie yet. He was now premier in the Mock Parliament, taking the portfolio of minister of finance. His 'government'
was instrumental in proposing resolutions for the union of New
Brunswick, Nova Scotia, and Prince Edward Island, which passed
the House by a vote of eleven to eight. A fortnight later Premier
Bennett incorporated Newfoundland into Confederation with
Canada. Alas for the fate of such progressive government! Premier
Bennett went on to propose full rights of citizenship to all un-
married women and widows (if qualified as to age and property).
Even this less-than-complete women's suffrage caused considerable debate; in the end, despite Bennett's eloquence, his government went down to defeat on it by fifteen to twelve. When
the new government attempted to bring in unrestricted reciprocity

with the United States, Dick Bennett, now leader of the opposition, sought to defeat it in a marathon speech of fifty-five minutes. That speech was, said the *Dalhousie Gazette*, 'the event of this parliament.' Notwithstanding Bennett's charges of clandestine annexationism, the government managed to hold on, by one vote, nine to eight.[42]

Dick Bennett had a gift for brilliant condensation; he had a forceful manner, and could be a dangerous opponent. His fellow students were, however, less impressed with him in Mock Parliament than in Moot Court. He lacked ductility, and the ability to parry, with wit and humour, the quick verbal thrust. Bennett was inclined to take thrusts seriously and sulk under them. But when roused he could be very effective. In Moot Court he impressed the students who worked alongside of him for his thoroughness in preparation and power of argument.[43]

Dick Bennett took his LL.B. degree at the Dalhousie Convocation of 25 April 1893. He would always retain a great affection for Dean Weldon, the law school, and for Dalhousie itself, their well-being one of his principal concerns as he grew older.

That summer of 1893 marked the beginning of Bennett's work as a full-time lawyer, admitted to the bar of New Brunswick, installed in the office in Tweedie's house at the western end of Chatham town, fronting the broad river. It was legal routine – leases, property, conveyances, the working business of a town lawyer – but with occasional appearances even at the New Brunswick Supreme Court. His pay was $600 a year, but no doubt a share of the fees would before long replace his salary. Tweedie had a lot to do; he was surveyor general of New Brunswick – a cabinet post – and in 1896 would be made provincial secretary. He was also a fair hand at other sorts of parties besides political. Max Aitken, who had become office boy at Tweedie's, gave Dick an account of a late December escapade over at Newcastle, whither Tweedie had gone on a case. Max had ended up there at a party at the Waverley Hotel, the leading watering hole. At 2 a.m. he and his friends were careering around the Newcastle streets in a sleigh. Tweedie and two others came up the hill in another sleigh behind a strong and lively horse;

We did not get off the road for them, and they had to take to the deep snow. The boss [Tweedie] swore black oaths and my blood curdled from very fear, lest the fire of the Lord should descend. He did not know us in the dark, and we told Allock [his driver] to go to h—l. Away in the distance we heard the strains of 'Nearer my God to Thee' floating through the air, followed by 'He laid her down upon the Grass' rendered by R.A. Lawlor, the others joining in the chorous [sic].

When last heard, Tweedie's group were in the snow singing 'Lead, kindly Light'! One can hear Dick chuckling over this. Max knew he loved a good story.[44]

In 1896 Chatham was given the status of a municipality and proceeded to have local elections. Max, a rambunctious seventeen, heard Dick Bennett wonder, half to himself, if he should stand for alderman. Max took this idea and ran with it; indeed, he did better than that, he bicycled with it, using Bennett's bicycle to scatter Bennett leaflets all through Queen's Ward. Bennett got in, 355 to 336.[45] A photograph of the first town council of Chatham shows a decidedly hirsute group, with Dick Bennett as the only clean-shaven one in the lot. Bennett earned a good reputation in that office, handling it with style, eloquence, grace, and dignity, according to one enthusiastic supporter.[46]

It looked as if Dick Bennett was fairly established in Chatham. Tweedie was busy with politics and provincial administration, Bennett was well-liked and respected in the town, and a pillar of the local Methodist church. Then came, as often in human affairs, chance and change.

In the summer of 1895 Dean Weldon had an inquiry from a fellow member of the Conservative caucus in Ottawa, Senator

James Lougheed of Calgary. Lougheed had been made a senator by Sir John A. Macdonald in 1889, and was looking for a new and energetic lawyer, perhaps for some official post, such as local crown attorney, something in the gift of the minister of the interior, T.M. Daly, with input from the minister of justice.[47] Weldon had not forgotten Dick Bennett who had helped him with his 1891 re-election, or his robust performance in the Dalhousie Mock Parliament, or his marks. What happened to the office Lougheed wanted to fill is not clear, but Lougheed's interest in Bennett continued, and he seems to have arranged to come to Chatham to meet him. Bennett was in no hurry to decide, but the terms tempted him. At Tweedie's he was getting $600 and free room and board; Lougheed offered full partnership and 20 per cent of the firm's earnings, up to $3,750 per year, with 30 per cent after that.[48] Besides, there were those lines of Whittier's,

> For of all sad words of tongue or pen,
> The saddest are these: 'It might have been!'

By the autumn of 1896, Dick Bennett had decided to go west.

Tweedie was sorry to see him go. The day Bennett decided to leave was a black day at Tweedie's house. But Tweedie understood the reasons; Bennett needed a bigger field 'for his pluck, vim and energy.'[49] Max Aitken felt worse, as did others. Max wrote while Bennett was at Hopewell Cape for Christmas, 'The office is very dull today, and an air of tranquillity rests on all the town. A disconsolate face and a ruffetted pink dress passed the window today. The lines on her face clearly showed that a young life had been blighted. I told her it was better to have loved and lost than never to have loved at all. Her only reply was a sigh.'[50]

Dick Bennett was given a farewell dinner at the Adams House, the main Chatham hotel, on Saturday night, 9 January 1897. He made a gracious speech, how he'd come as a stranger to the Miramichi and how much kindness and courtesy he had met, how fond he was of the Tweedies after six years of living with them. Now, he said, he would gratify ambition. 'Westward the star of empire takes its way,' he added, quoting Bishop Berkeley.[51]

J.L. Stewart, editor of the *Chatham World*, proposed the toast to the Bench and Bar, in a jocular style that probably amused Bennett but not all the lawyers:

People went to lawyers in trouble, and were soon in greater trouble ... The only good he could say of the profession, and the only thing that marred the guest of the evening, was that Mr. Bennett belonged to it. Lawyers pounced upon the estates of the deceased, and, with the help of the Judges, gobbled them up. Creditors who tried to get bankrupt estates out of the lawyers' hands were in danger of being made bankrupt themselves. Witnesses were browbeaten ... But it was necessary to keep on the good side of the profession ... in case one got entangled in legal toils, and hence this toast (laughter and applause).

As for the guest himself, Stewart said,

He was an honest man, but not too honest to prejudice the cause of a client by too much frankness of speech (Laughter). He was, though ardent and impulsive, a man of great caution. He was, in truth, so cautious, so habitually on guard against the danger of a hasty or premature utterance, that he rarely conversed with young ladies except by telephone. (Mr. Tweedie. – That's so. That's why I took my telephone out. Great laughter.) Ability and industry he has; but he has another even more important: he possessed gall, plenty of gall ... He must 'make by force his merit known' if he would 'clutch the golden keys' ... ability, industry and gall, the grand trinity of success.

Judge Wilkinson was more gracious. He noted that Bennett appeared before the New Brunswick Supreme Court the very day he was admitted to the New Brunswick bar, something quite unprecedented, and which abundantly vindicated his senior's confidence. The judge hoped that 'Calgarians would soon have reason to think that wise men still come from the east.'[52]

'Auld Lang Syne' sent the company home. The following day Dick Bennett left by train for Hopewell Cape. He did not forget to arrange for the binding of a new set of North-West Ordinances in Saint John, which he would pick up on his way west to Montreal and Calgary. That was on Saturday, 16 January 1897.

It was as if he had now set his face and his mind westward. His decision, with its appearance of hard rationality, was really instinctive. 'The decision you make at a particular moment is very often intuitive,' he said many years later. 'It is only as you get older you grow to use reason more.' Besides, he believed that a man had to expand his capacity to meet new and additional demands. If he did not, he would stand still.[53] There was something else. Dick Bennett had already come a long way, but he never forgot how hard it all was. 'I'll always remember the pit from which I was digged & the long uphill road I had to travel. I'll never forget one step.'[54]

2 〜◯

Work, Riches, and Empire: Calgary 1897-1927

WHEN DICK BENNETT STEPPED off the train in Calgary, on a bitter January morning in 1897, he encountered a ranch town of some four thousand inhabitants. There were some stone buildings, built of what the guidebook called 'a fine light-grey building stone,' giving the buildings 'a handsome and substantial appearance.'[1] But that 1905–6 perception of Calgary was an exaggerated version of what Bennett saw in 1897. What he remembered most was the biting wind at −40°F as he walked along the treeless streets from the station to the Alberta Hotel. Everyone knew he was coming, of course; Lougheed had gone through several law partners in recent years and it was known that a carefully chosen easterner was coming out. Dick Bennett had dressed as he always did. No cowboy stuff, then or later, for him: in well-cut clothes, cane, bowler hat, well-cared-for shoes, he would swing along the board sidewalks with a vigorous and jaunty gait. Lougheed had not bothered to meet the train; Calgarians usually did not in winter, for the prairie cold made trains almost invariably late. He and Dick met at 7 a.m. Dick's first evening there he heard a concert given by the Canadian soprano Marie-Louise Lajeunesse, otherwise known as Dame Emma Albani. She had retired from opera the year before, but she would continue to make Canadian tours until 1906. Dick remembered how cold the theatre was; Mme Albani had to be draped with a fur coat. A few nights later, going to Lougheed's place for dinner, Bennett almost lost his way in a blizzard. That was his introduction to Calgary social life, along with his attendance on his first Sunday in town at the local Methodist church.[2]

Of Calgary's inhabitants (numbering 4,865 in the 1901 census), 21 per cent were Methodist, 28 per cent Presbyterians, 27 per cent Anglicans, 12 per cent Catholics, 8 per cent Baptists, and 5 per cent Lutherans – the not untypical mix of a rising prairie town. According to one local wag, the population of Wetaskiwin, Alberta Territory, consisted of 287 souls and three total abstainers;[3] in Calgary there would have been a better proportion than that, something like 30 per cent of the population were against drink on principle. But there is no doubt that at least half of the population were enthusiasts the other way. The Alberta Hotel boasted of the longest bar in the West, and it was amply patronized. But Calgary was not the wild west town of old movies. The law required that bars be closed from 11:30 p.m. to 7 a.m. every weekday, and most of the weekend, from 7 p.m. on Saturday evening until 7 a.m. on Monday morning.[4] And, generally, the law was enforced, hence obeyed.

At first Calgary was not the land of opportunity that Lougheed had presented it to be. It was, Bennett said, 'a cow town of 4000 people and no business.' Not a few recent arrivals had moved on. It looked dead, the last place in the world where a man could make good, as Bennett put it.[5] He did not make $1,000 in his first year, or his second. His expenses were not high. His board and lodging in the Alberta Hotel came to $33 a month. Even so, living was more expensive than in New Brunswick. As he told a Hopewell Hill teacher thinking of coming west, renting houses in Calgary was expensive, about $30 a month, for they were scarce. Clothing was 15 per cent higher than in New Brunswick. A single man might get by on $50 a month back east, but would need $65 in Calgary.[6]

By 1900 things were going better. Dick Bennett was not a lone lawyer trying to grub up his own practice from scratch, but a partner in a well-established firm, and Lougheed, the senior partner, was the CPR solicitor in Calgary. Dick Bennett would not have left Tweedie's office in Chatham merely to fend for himself.[7] By 1903 he was making money, most of it in real estate. To people who constantly wrote him, he recommended the climate – it was everything that could be asked for; the only thing that bothered him personally was the wind, that he found 'very, very annoying.' He liked Alberta; he was becoming a Calgarian. Still, he would recommend that anyone who wanted to migrate come out first to look the ground over. The country was opening up rapidly, he told a correspondent from Berlin, Ontario: 'The fact is a young man with push and enterprise going into one of the towns along the line of railway while having to put up with great inconvenience will make more money in a year by speculating in real estate, and going in for life and fire insurance and a little law than he would make in five years in Ontario.'[8]

For pure law the Territories was not the best place to be but, as he put it to a colleague in Nanaimo, British Columbia, 'everyone in the legal profession on the main line from Calgary east was making money. The next five years will be years on unexampled progress in the Territories and I am quite certain that good money would easily be made by a capable and honest solicitor.'[9]

Note the appellation. That is what Bennett was himself. About his business practices there is ample evidence in his own papers and in Max Aitken's in London, England. And he was already giving some of his money away. He ordered, in April 1903, from the Methodist Book Room in Toronto, ten books for the little public library at Didsbury, Alberta, a small community some forty-four miles north of Calgary on the new railway to Edmonton. The books were Seton Thompson, *Biography of a Grizzly*; MacBeth's *Making of the Canadian West*; and four boys' books by G.A. Henty.[10] It was the beginning of a long history, Dick Bennett following Wesley's rule, 'give as much as you can.'

Calgary was attractive enough that his young Miramichi friend Max Aitken decided to follow his example and come west. Bennett had urged him to go into law, but Max's father was cautious. He wrote to Dick, grateful for his good influence on Max, and making a shrewd assessment of his obstreperous son:

His nature is such as would never make a first class student. It is too eager to grasp at the practical. And now that he has got a taste for business and a liking for the business intercourse of the world, I believe that he could no more set himself down to a course of theoretical study than he could take ... a journey to the moon ... Many, many thanks for your kind interest in Max! Your influence on him, in the past has, I know been very beneficial. Max is the better for having someone near him, to whom he can look with respect and for guidance. It would be selfish in me to express a desire that you had remained in Chatham. I cannot do that. – But had you remained here I feel certain that you would have imparted to Max ambitions and energies.[11]

That was in December 1897. A fortnight or so later Dick Bennett came east, on the way home for Christmas, stopping at Chatham en route. Within six months Max had flung himself west. He found his old friend living in one small room on the top floor of the Alberta Hotel, getting his meals in the hotel dining-room. Dick welcomed Max joyfully, for he was lonely; as Max noted, Dick's austerity, discipline, and ambition did not attract friends easily. Nor had his appearance much improved. He was still thin and lanky, well freckled, and desperately trying to put on weight to give his appearance a certain *embonpoint* that he associated with maturity. So Dick Bennett consumed huge meals; breakfasts of porridge, eggs and bacon, lots of toast and honey and marmalade, lunches and dinners in proportion.[12]

Max's adventures in Calgary did not consort well with a legal career. His will faltered. He had sworn off drinking and smoking the year before, but there is no evidence he was able to hold to that. 'If only your character equalled your ability!' Dick would say to him with an impatient sigh; and, he added, 'If only your industry equalled your energy!'[13] So instead of becoming a lawyer, Max bought a bowling alley. Dick was furious and for a time they were not on speaking terms. Dick Bennett could get like that when his moral sense was outraged. The bowling alley kept Max out of mischief for a time, for it tied him down every night. Eventually he got bored with it, went through an exchange, doubling his money. Dick and he made up; Max did what he had done in Chatham with his friend's first venture into public life as alderman – went to work for him in the November 1898 election to the Territorial legislature. Restless, impatient, Max drifted to Edmonton and invested in a large consignment of frozen meat that somehow got thawed. Max got burnt. There he met up again with a young New Brunswick lawyer from Bathurst called Jimmy Dunn, with whom he and Dick had shared more than one picnic on summer seashores on the Gulf of St Lawrence. Max believed that the West was the land of opportunity; Jimmy Dunn thought otherwise. 'The West must pay tribute to the East,' he said, 'and I'm off to the East where I can collect tribute.' In 1899 they both went back, Dunn to Montreal and Max to Halifax. Within two years they were both collecting tribute.[14]

Bennett stayed in the West and duly took his seat in the Territorial legislature at Regina. He was a maverick Conservative from the start. Independent, what might now be called a red Tory, he advocated workmen's compensation in 1899. He tried for the federal Parliament in the 1900 election against Frank Oliver and lost, but returned to the Territorial legislature in 1901, and would be re-elected in 1904. His acquaintance with Robert Borden of Nova Scotia, the new national leader of the Conservative party, may have been made back in Halifax; more likely it was made in the year of Borden's first trip west as national leader in 1902.

Borden was sixteen years older than Bennett, but they spoke a similar moral language. They came from villages not fifty miles apart, both sons of matriarchal mothers and feckless fathers. Both were school teachers who had crossed successfully into law. Both had strong social consciences, developed in King's County, Nova Scotia, and Albert County, New Brunswick; both believed that government enterprises could be efficient and effective – certainly they had no intrinsic fear of them. In both Nova Scotia and New Brunswick the earliest and most important railways came not because private enterprise wanted to build them, but because they wouldn't. The colonial governments built them, going into hock to do so. And they ran them: in Nova Scotia from Halifax to Windsor, Halifax to Truro; in New Brunswick from Shediac through Moncton to Saint John. Eventually they were subsumed under the aegis of the Intercolonial Railway, another government operation.

The ways and temperaments of Borden and Bennett were different. Borden spoke in a deep voice, slowly, half through his moustache (both Bennett and Eugene Forsey were wonderful at imitating Borden's voice and manner); Borden's words and thoughts were weighted, not to say ponderous, as if where Borden came from words were valuable commodities and there was lots of time in which to say them. Bennett spoke with a good, ringing voice, and with a torrent of words, with a rhetoric and rhythm that showed in his evening readings of the Bible, and his love of Whittier and Longfellow. Borden was a scholar, who read German and French, loved Goethe and Schiller, enjoyed birds and the outdoors, and was at the core of his being something of a poet himself. Bennett read and spoke French, but his was not a mind like Borden's; his taste in music gives him away, for he loved music with high emotional power with emphasis on the diapason, or songs that told a story.

Dick Bennett's scholarly instincts, whatever they might have been, had been partly transmuted into ambition and energy, into mastering law and making it serve his career to move out of Hopewell Cape toward the horizons of the great world. Borden was touched and moved by beauty in nature and in literature. Bennett could be reached by emotion too, but in more obvious, less rarified forms; his literary interests ran to biography and history which, he believed, had lessons to teach him. There were intellectual interests in Bennett. He read much; Monypenny and Buckle's six volumes on Disraeli he read and re-read, or Lecky's *Democracy and Liberty*; but these in a way served his cause, perhaps not in any direct perception of immediate use, but rather the elevation of his knowledge toward the sphere of life to which he was called. There is hardly a line in Bennett's letters about the beauty of the mountains and rivers of Alberta; there is much about their use in functional human terms.

Dick Bennett was driven by what he felt he had to do, and his full realization, never underestimated, that he had the capacity, intellect, and energy to do it. Unlike Borden, he was not much given to hesitations. In Dick's hand there is a gloss, perhaps for his Calgary Sunday school, on Genesis, chapter 7, the story of Noah and the ark. 'Did Noah hesitate? Did he say [to God] but I cannot undertake such work? Did he procrastinate? No. Fancy to yourself the scene: Far from the sea ... a gigantic mass of wood and iron.' It is not a bad example, either, of Dick as a teacher. He was more a solitary soul than Borden, carrying the burdensome but rejuvenating Methodist belief in redemption even in this world. He was dominated by the four great Protestant principles, as he once put it, of Hard Work, Honesty, Righteousness, and Temperance.[15]

There emerges from the correspondence of Bennett with Borden something of the policies of both. Borden sought to bring Dick Bennett's instinctive independence under some control, urging him to work with Frederick Haultain, the Conservative premier of the North-West Territories. That was not going to be exactly easy, for Haultain saw Regina as the future capital of a great single western province extending from the Manitoba border to the Rockies. Dick Bennett thought there ought to be at least two new provinces, and certainly Calgary the capital of one of them. He also felt Haultain's loyalty to the party questionable; although Haultain was a good Conservative, he would keep appointing Liberals.[16] Borden refused to take sides and at the Moose Jaw Conservative convention of 25 March 1903 the difficulty was patched up, mostly by concentrating on the prior issue – responsible (that is, provincial) government for the Territories, together with full control of their own budget and especially their natural resources, not least of which was the land itself.[17] It was a useful, smoothing-out operation. Now, Dick Bennett told Borden, American settlers would stop wondering why Conservatives fought each other on local issues and agreed on dominion ones.[18]

Railways had become the other staple theme of western politics. In prospect, in 1903, were *two* additional transcontinental railways besides the Canadian Pacific: the Canadian Northern and the Grand Trunk. Bennett's views on transportation came partly from his New Brunswick experience. He had no objection to government railways. It seemed sensible to him that two new competing railways, both looking to charters, money, and land grants, could be sorted out by being combined in a government railway. Associated with it in Bennett's mind was the tariff. The West, he said, could live with Borden's policy of 'adequate protection' for Canadian workers and Canadian industry, but along with that had to be 'a strong national transportation policy.'[19] The West could accept the former on condition of the latter. Certainly Canada could not support three transcontinental railway lines. The West also wanted railway rates to be government-controlled. It still cost westerners too much to get their wheat to seaboard. Until that was solved, Bennett said, there will be constant agitation in the Territories. As to a government railway as such, it ought to be an improvement on the Intercolonial Railway, which had had too much politics mixed up in it. 'If a Government railroad could be built to the west and be placed in the hands of a strong Commission and absolutely beyond political control it would serve the desired purpose.'[20]

Bennett developed this argument further in August 1904, making suggestions to Borden for his electoral address in the autumn general election. It was in effect Bennett's version of the National Policy: to build the supremacy of the Canadian workshop, develop factories, all of which would have spin-off advantages for western farmers and ranchers. As for the railways, 'we are not warranted in granting large blocks of land or paying large subsidies to private corporations.' Adequate facilities at least cost was

Bennett's aim, at the same time keeping as far as possible absolute control over freight rates in the hands of the people.[21]

Bennett had also asked Borden if, in his electoral address that autumn, he would mention Joseph Chamberlain's argument that 'the strength and permanency of the Empire, not less than our attachment to it, consists in the adjustment of the fiscal relations of the Colonies to one another and to the Motherland.' Borden did.[22] Dick Bennett's passionate attachment to the idea of the British Empire was not the naive devotion of a United Empire Loyalist. His imperialism was a form of Canadian nationalism writ large. It had the advantage of not only encompassing within it Canadian expansion, but that of Britain's empire as well. Its frontiers were vast: Australia, India, Egypt, South Africa, the West Indies; they were an extension of Canada's. In Sara Jeannette Duncan's 1904 novel, *The Imperialist*, the hero, Lorne Murchison, like Dick Bennett, is caught by the greatness of the British imperial idea; it was not just crude expansionism as such (that was for Germans!) but the highest and noblest calling of the human race, in its cleanest and most disinterested form. And if England in the future should become tired and effete, there was Canada, young and resolute, to take over. The question, as Lorne Murchison put it, was that of the whole stamp and character of Canadian future existence; '... is it to be our own stamp and character, acquired in the rugged discipline of our colonial youth, and developed in the national usage of the British Empire?' Thus Paardeberg, in the South African War (February 1900), was a Canadian victory, and not just because Canadian troops were there and luckily won the battle.[23]

Canadian response to the Boer War was not adventitious: it had been created by two decades of increasingly powerful linkages. Little boys even in the 1920s would recite,

The twenty-fourth of May
Is the Queen's birthday,

If you don't give us a holiday
We'll all run away.

The idea of the glory of Anglo-Saxondom was set out brilliantly by Joseph Chamberlain to the Toronto Board of Trade in December 1887:

... I should think our patriotism was warped and stunted indeed if it did not embrace the Greater Britain beyond the seas – (cheers) – the young and vigorous nations carrying everywhere throughout the globe a knowledge of the English tongue and English love of liberty and law ... Still less am I inclined to make any distinction between these interests of Englishmen at home and Englishmen in Canada and Australia. (Cheers) ... You cannot if you would break the invisible bond which binds us together. (Cheers) Their forefathers are our forefathers. They worshipped at our shrines. They sleep in our churchyards ... We are all branches of one family.[24]

In 1885 the Canadian government had no intention of getting involved in any British campaign to reconquer the Egyptian Sudan; but in the Boer War of 1899 vociferous public opinion in English Canada forced the Laurier government to send Canadian contingents to South Africa. The reason for the difference was that many English Canadians had been educated to the idea of a British empire, to the glory of an empire on which the sun never set. It was represented vividly, in wonderful Mercator projection, on the stamp issued by Laurier's postmaster general, William Mulock, in December 1898. It celebrated imperial penny postage, with red all over the map of the world and Canada right in the centre.

The same idea was embedded in important ways in the school systems of English Canada. The most prevalent of all textbooks in the four Atlantic provinces were the Royal Readers. They were published by Nelson's from the mid-1870s onward, and were soon the authorized and graded readers for school children in Britain, British colonies overseas, and the Canadian provinces. Readers I to VI presented readings from British history and literature. One poem appears in all the provincial readers, from the mid-1880s onward in Number V, 'The Triumph of the English Language,' by J.G. Lyons. It is the only long poem that I have seen transcribed in the Bennett Papers. He undoubtedly taught it in Douglastown as part of the public school curriculum of New Brunswick, as it was in Nova Scotia and Newfoundland.[25] That poem is a striking glimpse into the luxurious innocence, the naive nobility, of Anglo-Saxon imperial ideas pitched at the level of grade eight:

Now gather all our Saxon bards, let harps and hearts be strung,
To celebrate the triumphs of our own good Saxon tongue;
For stronger far than hosts that march with battle-flags unfurled,
It goes with FREEDOM, THOUGHT, and TRUTH, to rouse and rule the
world.

Stout Albion learns its household lays on every surf-worn shore,
And Scotland hears its echoing far as Orkney's breakers roar –
From Jura's crags and Mona's hills it floats on every gale,
And warms with eloquence and song the homes of Innisfail.

On many a wide and swarming deck it scales the rough wave's
crest,
Seeking its peerless heritage – the fresh and fruitful West;
It climbs New England's rocky steeps, as victor mounts a throne;
Niagara knows and greets the voice, still mightier than its own.

It spreads where Winter piles deep snows on bleak Canadian plains,
And where on Essequibo's banks eternal Summer reigns;
It glads Acadia's misty coasts, Jamaica's glowing isle,

And bides where, gay with early flowers, green Texan prairies
  smile;
It tracks the loud swift Oregon, through sunset valleys rolled,
And soars where Californian brooks wash down their sands of gold
  ...

Tasmania's maids are wooed and won in gentle Saxon speech;
Australian boys read Crusoe's life by Sydney's sheltered beach;
It dwells where Afric's southmost capes meet oceans broad and
  blue,
And Nieuvald's rugged mountains gird the wide and waste karroo.

It kindles realms so far apart, that while its praise you sing
These may be clad with Autumn's fruits, and those with flowers of
  Spring;
It quickens lands whose meteor lights flame in an Arctic sky,
And lands for which the Southern Cross hangs its orbed fires on
  high ...

Take heed, then, heirs of Saxon fame! take heed, nor once disgrace
With deadly pen or spoiling sword, our noble tongue and race.
Go forth prepared in every clime to love and help each other,
And judge that they who counsel strife would bid you smith – a
  brother.

Go forth, and jointly speed the time, by good men prayed for long,
When Christian States, grown just and wise, will scorn revenge and
  wrong;
When Earth's oppressed and savage tribes shall cease to pine or
  roam,
All taught to prize these English words – FAITH, FREEDOM, HEAVEN,
  and HOME.

Dick Bennett's beliefs comprehended not a little of all that, but
they also derived sustenance from his extensive reading and

teaching of British and Canadian history. His own inheritance was part of it: his ancestors on both sides were pre-Loyalist Yankee; his mother's great-grandfather had fought at Louisburg. For Dick Bennett, the Armada, the victories of the Seven Years' War, the battles of Trafalgar and Waterloo, were part of a swelling paean of imperial achievement. He gloried in it. His favourite song became, and would remain, 'Land of Hope and Glory,' music by Sir Edward Elgar, words by Arthur Benson:

> Land of Hope and Glory, Mother of the Free
> How can we extol thee, who are born of thee?
> Wider still and wider shall thy bounds be set,
> God who made thee mighty, make thee mightier yet.

He might even have accepted the vainglory in 'The Soldiers of the Queen':

> And when we say we've always won,
> And when they ask us how it's done,
> We'll proudly point to every one
> Of England's Soldiers of the Queen!

Thus, if Whittier and Longfellow spoke to Bennett's New Brunswick environment, geographic and religious, his sense of history ministered to his British inheritance, to his feeling of belonging to a wider empire even than Canada's frontiers on three oceans. To quote the words on the 1898 Canadian stamp: 'We Hold a Vaster Empire than Has Been.'

Dick Bennett was at Hopewell Cape for Christmas 1903; he was busy, and making money, but he wanted to talk to Max about the imperial initiatives under the Balfour government. Arthur Balfour was the prime minister, but the real leader of the party was the much more energetic Joseph Chamberlain. He was campaigning for commercial union between Britain and her dominions and colonies. Max was then in Halifax, just getting started with Royal Securities Corporation, the first bond-selling corporation in eastern Canada. (Note the name!) John F. Stairs, president of the Union Bank and leading Halifax financier, and R.B. Bennett were both Aitken mentors, and all three were enthusiasts for Joseph Chamberlain's policies. In Dick's crowded schedule he managed to squeeze in two days with Max in Halifax over the new year. They talked continually about the possibility of realizing Chamberlain's imperial vision. They saw themselves together one day in an imperial Parliament; the idea of empire led them on, as the Lord had led the children of Israel out of Egypt, so Bennett put it, by day in a pillar of cloud, by night in a pillar of fire. Max saw Dick off on the train at the old North Street station, invigorated and heartened by his visit, saddened by his departure. 'How I liked and admired him!'[26]

Bennett never abandoned those central beliefs in the power and the future of the British Empire. Nine years later, when Borden's naval aid bill came before the House of Commons, Dick was the member for Calgary. He intervened late in the debate, the subject virtually exhausted. He proceeded to liven it up with a ringing assertion of Canada's imperial responsibilities. This naval aid to Britain embodied a principle that Bennett had supported all his life. What is Canada's navy now, in February 1913? he asked. 'We have nothing but the *Niobe*, *Rainbow* and the *Minnie M.*' (This last was a dig at the Liberals at Sault Ste Marie who had imported forty voters from Sault Ste Marie, Michigan.) The naval aid bill simply recognized 'the duty that devolves upon us, as citizens of the British Empire, to do everything we can for the common defence.' We are, after all, an integral part of the Empire and the bill aims in the long run at a great principle: 'the creation of an Imperial Parliament that, with men from this Dominion, and from that dominion, from New Zealand, Australia and Canada, would legislate upon every subject that effects [*sic*] the common rights and common well-being of this great Empire.' It was all very well for Sir Wilfrid Laurier to offer beautiful generalities about the freedom Canada enjoyed under the British flag. What had Canada done to earn it? They had bought a *Niobe* and a *Rainbow*! 'Faith without works,' asserted Bennett – he was good at assertion – 'is dead, dead, dead.' The British people paid five pence in the pound as interest on the capital Britain had spent on Canada; should we not pay something? Do Canadians, as the Liberals assert, owe *nothing* to England? Where the British flag has gone, 'there has followed order, justice, freedom, equality under the law.' Did that count for nothing? 'I was thinking just this morning,' Bennett said, 'of Browning's trip homeward bound from the Mediterranean, as he was passing Cape St Vincent:

"Here and here did England help me,
How can I help England?" say ...'

The Canadian contribution to an imperial navy was like a contribution to a common dyke: the Liberals were saying, 'I'm tired of contributing to his sea dyke; my marsh is miles away, I'll build a side one of my own.' Then came a great gale, a huge tide, and both dykes went. 'Hon. gentlemen prattle about a Canadian navy, they talk about the navy they will build sometime in the future while the dyke ... vanishes.'[27]

There was more to Bennett's argument than that Bay of Fundy metaphor about dykes. There was the problem of immigrants. Canada needed some principle outside of herself to help develop the loyalties of a great and diversified immigrant population. It was especially a western Canadian problem: in the last seven years, Bennett said, some seven hundred thousand people had come to Canada, of whom less than 30 per cent were British. The others had come 'without knowledge of our history, with little regard for our traditions, caring nothing for our glorious past and asking us for a national ideal, some aspiration, some ambition, some hope by which they may be led.'[28]

All past empires sooner or later had come to ruin. Lord Curzon in India had noted the old ruins when he had first come to Delhi; the insurance that the British Empire would not suffer the same fate was binding the self-governing colonies to the mother country. In such a great federation there would be the further vision, a wider hope, 'that one day the Dominion [of Canada] will be the dominant factor in that great federation, when we may be able as the dominant partner to protect the destinies of the race and breed to which we belong.'[29]

Bennett would never get over this wonderful vision. As late as May 1947 he was extolling it; Britain having extended the principle of self-government to colonies overseas, the corollary was that the nations of the 1947 Commonwealth should take up the idea of Joseph Chamberlain – a common attitude to common problems on which the common life of the Commonwealth depended. The Ottawa conference of 1932, Bennett said, was an attempt to do just that.[30]

Dick Bennett and Max Aitken worked together towards this most of their lives. There were certainly quarrels and interruptions: a cold letter from Bennett early in 1914 began 'My dear Sir.' That was about Max trying to make Bennett's name big in the financial world; Bennett was more concerned with having a good name than a big one.[31] There was a serious quarrel in 1930 when Bennett felt aggrieved over a Toronto *Globe* interview with Beaverbrook in which Max praised King's 1930 budget for its improved tariff preferences to Britain. The interview was given in May 1930; the Toronto *Globe*, in a nasty bit of trickery, published it in July, in the midst of the election campaign. Bennett was, not unreasonably, furious; he did not know the interview was two months old. Beaverbrook went to some pains to show how the error had arisen; Bennett was not appeased, not then.

Then out of the blue, in October 1930, he arrived in London and patched it up.[32] Beaverbrook was, and would remain, Bennett's most devoted friend and supporter throughout Bennett's life. And, for that matter, afterwards.

Bennett and Aitken both aimed at financial independence, to get enough capital to live comfortably from the income. But neither was content with that; Max liked to wrestle with life, as he put it once, 'to dare and win.'[33] Bennett wanted to achieve things, reach goals, change the political complexion of the British Empire. Max was volatile and easily bored; he was like a builder who, once his building was successfully up and going, wanted to go on to something new. Bennett had sterner grit than that; he had determination and tenacity, and he did not mind hard roads – he had come a lot farther along one than Max. So Dick worked, days and nights, with that powerful combination of energy and application, made efficient – oiled one might say – by a capacious and exact memory. Learning, and remembering what he had learnt, came effortlessly to Dick Bennett. As for work, that was something the Methodist ethic had long ago taught him.

He was an upright and honourable businessman, loyal and faithful to his clients, honest as daylight. He would not, however, be put upon, by governments, by opponents, by anyone. Nor, if there were injustice, would he accept it. There is an interesting example that illustrates his early labour sympathies. In July 1902 the carpenters of Calgary struck against the local Contractors' Association, for a nine-hour day and a minimum wage of $2.50 a day. The contractors asked for a six-month deferral of that demand; the union offered to arbitrate, but the contractors refused. That struck Bennett as high-handed and unfair. There was an evening protest meeting, the major speech given by Bennett, 'in hearty sympathy,' as he put it, with the carpenters. Bennett urged the working men of Calgary to become members of labour unions; he would do all in his power 'to aid labour organizations in making just demands which would build up homes for them and make strong, reliant citizens.' That suggests the bourgeois direction of his sympathy, but it does not make it any less real. He was the hero of the evening.[34]

Bennett was not a party man, in the sense of my party right or wrong. He believed in party government, but only up to the point where it did not cross his principles. From his early years in the Territorial legislature in Regina he was rather a maverick, or at the very least an independent-minded Conservative. When he got into the Alberta legislature in 1909 he was the same. He did not think much of it – a glorified town council – and he became rather the lone wolf in Edmonton. There were only three Conservatives anyway in the forty-one-seat House. But when it came to really hitting out, there was no one in the Alberta House to touch him. His 1910 speech on the Great Waterways Scandal was a sensation.[35]

In August 1911 he was asked to stand for the dominion Parliament. He had been confident in 1904 that he would end up in the House of Commons, but by 1911 he was so busy that he accepted the nomination for Calgary with great reluctance. On 21 September 1911 he swept the polls, with a 2,500-vote majority. Parliament opened on 17 November 1911, and Bennett, as the most senior and experienced member from the West, was given the honour of moving the address in reply to the speech from the throne. That was all very well; but within three weeks Dick was tired of Parliament and all its works. It had no place for him; he was a mere backbencher, voting when called upon. There was not nearly enough for him to do. He should have been in cabinet.[36] But Borden had Senator James Lougheed as his minister without portfolio, and could not have two Alberta men in cabinet – let alone two from Calgary, and from the same law firm! So Dick Bennett chafed at inaction, at the lack of recognition for his past work and present talents.

He was also impatient of party discipline and none too willing to follow caucus. One of the best examples of his powerful punch and his independence of party was his strong opposition in the House of Commons in 1914 to his party's commitment to bailing out, for the second time in two years, the Canadian Northern Railway. He began with Thomas Babington Macaulay's farewell address at Edinburgh in 1857:

I acknowledge great errors and deficiencies but I have nothing to acknowledge inconsistent with rectitude of intention and independence of spirit ... that I have honestly desired the happiness and prosperity and greatness of my country; that my course, right or wrong, was never determined by any selfish or sordid motive.

There followed a massive, well-documented, four-hour denunciation of Mackenzie and Mann and all their works; it did not exclude denunciation of Meighen, the solicitor general, who was piloting the Canadian Northern Railway loan through the House. Meighen's 'impertinent interruptions' annoyed Bennett; he denounced him as 'the gramophone of Mackenzie and Mann.' Bennett admitted having failed in his duty in 1913 in not breaking party ranks over the Canadian Northern loan of that year. But he would not repeat that error in 1914.[37]

He hated injustice, such as the heavy-handed application of the Military Service Act in Calgary in 1918. He threw himself into the fight against the Conservative government's interpretation of the act, arguing that the parliamentary resolution ending exemptions for agricultural workers was *ultra vires* of the powers given by the acts of 1914 and 1917. He fought it all the way to the Supreme Court of Canada. And lost.[38]

He was an early advocate of workmen's compensation. His first speech in the House of Commons, on 20 November 1911, in moving the address in reply, made patent his concern for industrial accidents. He thought the dominion government should have a department of public health to supervise such questions: '... the largest number of industrial accidents happened toward the close

of the day's work when the vital forces are low, and too many
of our railway accidents have been directly attributable to the
employees remaining too long on duty.'[39]

Like Borden, Bennett wanted controversial questions put in the
hands of independent government commissions. A tariff commission would, he said, 'lift the tariff out of politics.' Bennett
wanted firmer control of corporations, making the point that if
legislatures issued charters it was their responsibility to see that
these charters were observed. It was the basic distinction between
unlimited and limited liability:

... if men meet together and conclude to enter partnership, the limit of
their responsibility is the limit of their joint and several fortunes. But
when they constitute themselves into a joint stock company, or corporation, the limit of their liability is the amount of their subscriptions.
Every corporation is the creature of a statute, and the statute expresses
in some way the will of the people through their legislatures. If that
be so, and if there be certain immunities and rights and privileges
which flow to men who constitute themselves into corporations, it fol-
lows that the parliament or legislature that created them, that gave
them birth and existence, has the power to impose upon them limitations commensurate with the demands and necessities of the people.[40]

There should be a tribunal controlling the issue of securities that
would protect the public. He insisted that a tribunal should have
control over the capitalization of industrial concerns, so that the
stock issued have some just proportion to the assets and value
of the enterprise.[41]

Social legislation was not at all strange to Maritime Conservatives such as Bennett and Borden. Bennett approved of Borden's
Halifax platform of 1907, with its strong emphasis on government
ownership, a non-partisan civil service, national telephones and
telegraphs; indeed, his own ideas on railway policy were reflected
in it. Bennett also liked King's idea of old age pensions when it

came before Parliament in 1926, though he felt the legislation had been too hastily conceived. He wanted a contributory system, not a unilateral dole, except for those who could not make contributions. Furthermore, King's proposed pensions required the cooperation of the provinces. To do otherwise would be 'imposing our will upon the provincial legislatures.' Unemployment insurance he supported as well in 1927, again with a contributory system to encourage thrift and industry.

Perhaps his most innovative idea in 1927 was one which, he said, was not original with him but came from Sir Edmund Walker, president of the Canadian Bank of Commerce from 1907 to 1924, and a protean man of letters. It was, in effect and intention, a goods and services tax; everyone who bought anything would pay a percentage levy. 'It is simple, it is universal, it is convenient, it is equal, it is easily collected – it has all the qualifications that were mentioned by the late Adam Smith.'[42]

The direction of these utterances, their social thrust, was not new in Bennett; they were, on the contrary, old and familiar positions.

The history of Richard Bedford Bennett as a businessman develops naturally from that context. Unregenerate capitalist he was not. He was certainly a most scrupulous one. He most certainly made money, and by means that one might now designate as insider trading. But in the business canons of the time, it was entirely legitimate and wholly honourable. It was proper to take advantage of inside knowledge, provided it involved no betrayal of confidence, no violation of a lawyer's relations with his client, no dishonouring of obligations or, still more, not living up to the letter of one's word. Dick Bennett and John Stairs, in their several ways, taught those mighty lessons to Max Aitken, and he took them seriously. In business your word was your bond; it was, indeed, your most precious asset. Max learnt that.[43]

Max often confided frankly his troubles to Dick; he cheerfully solicited information, advice, whatever help he wanted, whenever he felt he needed it. Dick, lawyer that he was, was more chary the other way; he rarely asked Max to do anything for him. Max wanted to buy Calgary Milling Company, and as usual was impatient for facts. Do you recommend purchase of Calgary Milling? he asked. What are the prospects of the company? Bennett replied cautiously, that it's not easy to get inside boardrooms. 'I have learned to be extremely careful in the statements I make in any way dealing with financial matters,' he added, rather as if he were a thirty-nine-year-old lecturing a thirty-year-old, which is what it really was. 'What I try to do is to give you information that is strictly accurate.'[44] There spoke the corporate lawyer!

Dick Bennett's scrupulousness is revealed in a confidential letter to Max about the purchase of Rocky Mountain Cement in 1910. The idea was to buy up the common stock and sell it to Canada Cement at a profit. When Max wired Bennett and asked him to be Canada Cement's lawyer, Bennett at once gave up acquiring Rocky Mountain Cement stock for himself; he did not propose to 'depart from my fixed rules in connection with this transaction, vague and indefinite though my relations might be to the Merger [Canada Cement] ...' But, he told Max, watch the price; they want to charge you $600,000 for a $400,000 property. You don't need $200,000 worth of water.[45]

Exshaw was a still more notorious example, where Sir Sandford Fleming and his friends created $4 million worth of watered stock and filched $200,000 of bond money.[46] It did not help that Fleming's useless son was secretary of the company. The difference between Canada Cement and Exshaw was, Max said, the difference between honesty and dishonesty. Fleming's attempt to unload Exshaw onto Canada Cement outraged Bennett:

When I consider the extent and character of the claims preferred against the Exshaw Company, the manner in which its business was transacted and the properties which were unloaded upon it by Fleming and his friends, I cannot but conclude that a parliamentary investigation sufficiently wide in its scope could not but fail to destroy absolutely the small remnant of respect that remains in the minds of the business men of Canada for this old man.[47]

When Fleming tried to raise the issue with Borden, Bennett briefed Borden on the full story. By December 1911 the cement question was dead, and around Ottawa the impression was growing that Fleming was crazy. 'And I think,' said Dick, 'a kinder method of disposing of him could not be suggested.'[48]

He was by this time a well-known figure in Calgary, walking in his frock coat, with hat and cane, to the Methodist Church, usually for evening service, not being an enthusiastic early riser. Calgarian he was, and thought himself so to be; that he was an unusual one did not bother him. R.G. Brett, a doctor at Banff, and later lieutenant-governor of Alberta, once said to him, 'Bennett, you're an astonishing young man. There's no one your equal in Western Canada. In my opinion you're going to be prime minister of Canada ... But, Bennett, why in hell can't you be like other men? Stanley,' said Brett, turning to G.F.G. Stanley's father, 'he was everlastingly studying ... there was no sense of sport in him.' Dick Bennett did not worry about that. His style was his own.[49]

John Brownlee, later premier of Alberta, joined Bennett's firm in 1909, walking in off the street. He was impressed with the tremendous amount of work Bennett did. Bennett gave his instructions so rapidly that Brownlee had to sit down on the office steps to figure it all out. At night he and a colleague studied for their bar exams; Dick Bennett frequently came in and would say, 'Well boys, what's the subject tonight?' Then he would pace up and down the office and give them a lecture. 'He seemed to remember every case in law,' said Brownlee, 'he could quote paragraph upon paragraph, virtually verbatim, from any textbook, and often from obscure books that did not enter into law.'[50]

Dick Bennett lived modestly enough. After an initial sojourn at the Alberta Hotel he moved to a rooming house at 222 4th

Avenue West, owned by Sarah Smith, a widow. There he stayed put for fifteen years. By 1905 he could have bought a dozen houses, but he was comfortable there and, taking his meals at the Alberta Hotel for $50 a month, saw no reason to change. It was only in 1923 that he moved, first to the Ranchman's Club for a year, then to a suite in the Palliser Hotel.[51]

His connections with local worthies were considerable. Some of them were his rivals at the bar, such as Peter McCarthy, both in court and in politics; not a few lawyers disliked Bennett's immense knowledge and his ill-concealed pride in it. But there came to be a Bennett Table at the back of the dining-room in the Alberta Hotel, where he dined with local cronies from ranching, real estate, and the Hudson's Bay Company. He had for a time a well-publicized feud with Bob Edwards, a drunken Scottish journalist of great talent, who had ended up in Calgary and published an amusing, if scurrilous, weekly called the *Eye-Opener*.

For several years the *Eye-Opener* liked to bait the CPR and since Bennett was the railway's solicitor, he did not escape. It was quite possible that Edwards's opposition helped tip the balance against Bennett in the 1905 first provincial election in Alberta, when Bennett lost by twenty-nine votes. The feud was cleverly patched up by Paddy Nolan, a famous trial lawyer, and others, and by 1909 Bob Edwards had become an habitué at the Bennett Table. Dick Bennett, who had a lively appreciation of Edwards's humour, would regale him with modest stories which, Bennett said, would hardly be suitable for the 'Great Moral Weekly,' but which amused him. An example of a Bennett story: a CPR train ran down five horses belonging to Shorty McLaughlin of High River, and killed them. Shorty wanted Paddy Nolan to act for him in suing for damages. 'Did the CPR train actually run down those horses?' Paddy asked. Shorty assured him of the fact. 'Well,' Paddy said, 'I'm sorry, Shorty, but I can't take that case. Any horses that can't outrun a CPR train are better dead. You're lucky to be rid of them.'[52] Alice Millar told a *Toronto Star Weekly* reporter in 1938,

'I only wish that you could hear him out in Calgary talking with
some of the old timers. Such yarn swapping and laughter ...'[53]
Edwards came to admire Dick Bennett's humour, his vitality and
determination, whiskyless though he was. He hoped that the
absence of whisky would not allow microbes to get at him and
bring him to an early grave. In 1909 the *Eye-Opener* helped elect
Bennett to the Alberta legislature, and even more in 1911 to the
House of Commons.

One lasting feud was with the local Liberal paper, the Calgary
Albertan. W.M. Davidson, the editor, had not given Bennett much
mercy. The *Albertan* had hired a new cub reporter, Chester Bloom,
who had not heard of the feud, or indeed hardly heard of Bennett.
Davidson, making mischief no doubt, sent Bloom to get an interview from Bennett. The young reporter duly knocked on Bennett's door at 4th Avenue West. It was jerked open. 'What do
you want?' said Bennett, not pleased at being interrupted in whatever he was doing. The young man got out four words: 'Interview
for the *Albertan* ...,' when he was blasted with a tremendous
tirade. Bloom, said Bennett, was a devil in human form, an em-
issary from that worse and bigger devil, Davidson, who was hid-
ing behind his inkpot; and both were out to blacken the reputations
of decent citizens.

'Just a minute, just a minute now,' I shouted an octave above him,
'I've only been in your town three days. I don't think much of it, and
of you either.'
'Where did you come from?' asked R.B., instantly cooling off.
'From Seattle,' I admitted, adding, 'I don't know anything about
Calgary politics and care a darn sight less.'
'Come in,' he said politely. It was a delightful talk. He grew more
genial and mellow as he went along, gave me some valuable instruc-
tion on Canadian and Alberta politics, winding up with a first class
quotable column of Ottawa political gossip. The only thing I didn't get
was a drink.[54]

A teetotaller, charged to it by his mother, Dick Bennett came in later years to offer drinks, and wine, as civilized hosts were apt to do; but he did not touch alcohol himself. Or not quite. In time he came to enjoy the flavour of sherry in consommé believing, perhaps rightly, that the heat had burned off the alcohol. There were Calgary stories that he liked rum baba for dessert, the alcohol presumably suffering the same fate. He liked crème de menthe over ice cream, alleged it had alcohol in it only as a preservative.

Bennett was a Calgary Canadian. He named the 'American Hill' Mount Royal, got its streets named Montcalm, Sydenham, Quebec, Durham, and others. The view that Bennett was always a New Brunswicker, that he could never be a Calgarian wearing eastern clothes (and fairly formal ones at that), or without drinking, smoking, and swearing, may have something in it, but not very much. Bennett's appearance was his own style, merely the carapace of his character. Bennett thought of himself as Calgarian. It was his home; it was where he had made his way in the world. In October 1927 he reflected that he had lived thirty years in Calgary, had seen it grow from four thousand to seventy-four thousand citizens; his life had become thoroughly embedded in it. Even the iron bridge that brought the Canadian Pacific and its trains across the Bow River, just below Calgary, had its echoes in his experience; it was a symbol of Calgary and all that it meant. It was an emotional thing with him, and emotionally did he describe it:

I have lived with it, grown with it, thought with it, expanded with it, and I have loved it. I have never crossed that bridge as I have night after night, and I have travelled much over it, I have never crossed that river and heard the roll of the wheels of the car as they crossed the bridge without a little quickening of the throb of my heart, because it spelled to me the place I call my home, the people with whom I live.[55]

Southern Alberta, with its great swales of grassland, had become Bennett's country. It was a world of long horizons, different but analogous to those of the Bay of Fundy in Albert County, the one land, the other sea. The drama of that Alberta landscape was the sky, filled with light and distances. The world of Calgary was wide; one could think of what lay beyond. The western horizon was piled up with the Rockies, the glistening spine of the whole continent. But eastward perspectives and duties, political and moral, opened.

3

Mildred Bennett, Hazel Colville, and the Wages of Power and Exile

1927-1947

R.B. BENNETT had been MP for Calgary from 1911 to 1917, and again since 1925, and would remain so until January 1939. His Calgary law practice had become of less importance, especially since the death of Mrs E.B. Eddy in 1921 forced him to look after the affairs of the Eddy Company more and more. Bennett was not a managing director, but he and Mrs Eddy's brother, Harry Shirreff, were close to being so. With Harry Shirreff's death in May 1926, Bennett became the majority shareholder of the company, his 1,508 shares of Eddy's stock worth nearly $2 million at that time. Bennett probably had nearly as much accumulated in other investments. On the board of Metropolitan Life of New York, and of the Royal Bank of Canada, Bennett was a wealthy man.

Arthur Meighen resigned as prime minister on 25 September 1926, eleven days after the election, and his leadership of the party two weeks later. The Conservative party shook itself, appointed Hugh Guthrie as interim leader for the coming session, and finally resolved to have a convention, something it had been considering for seven years. It was to meet in Winnipeg on Monday, 10 October 1927. R.B. Bennett professed no great interest, and indeed he had his hands full looking after Eddy's, plus his presidency of Royalite, whose well No. 4 had just blown in at Turner Valley, at five hundred barrels a day. He could well ignore calls for his nomination. There were other candidates; Hugh Guthrie was already off and making speeches. The Liberal *Toronto Star* reminded its readers of camels finding it difficult to go through eyes of needles, although that was a bit much from Joe Atkinson's paper; he was wealthier than Bennett was.[1]

R.B. put off a decision, did not declare himself. His early ambitions, back in the days at Chatham, whatever newspapers might say, had focused within much narrower limits than being in the running, as he now had to contemplate, for being the next prime minister of Canada. Providence had been good to him, he had worked hard, but he did not really feel fitted for this new role.

It finally came down to a question of obligation, 'to the country that has done so much for me.' So many people had written to him, he wrote later to Alma Russell, that he would find 'comfort and cheer in the dark days that are before me.'[2] Thus, solaced by his friends and stiffened by his Canadian nationalism, Bennett shouldered the burden. That Canadian theme he echoed in a speech to the Winnipeg Rotary Club the day the convention opened. 'The first thing we must do in this country is to build up a strong national consciousness – a virile Canadianism – we have suffered from an inferiority complex long enough.' How was that to be done? A beginning should be made with radio. Canada was swamped with American radio, American examples, institutions, commercialism. Here indeed, as Grattan O'Leary noted, was 'a Tory of the Left.'[3]

At the convention he struck a middle course between his Canadian nationalism and his imperialism, seeking to unite the left and right wings of the party. He was the golden boy, rich and talented, and best of all, a westerner with Maritime roots. Well ahead on the first ballot with 40 per cent of the votes, he was elected on the second ballot. He would eventually appoint three of the most popular of his rivals to his 1930 cabinet: Hugh Guthrie, the nearest, would become minister of justice; C.H. Cahan, the next, his secretary of state; and Dr R.J. Manion, the third rival, would be minister of railways. In the meantime, between 1927 and 1930 he spent much effort, successful mostly, to build up the party. In the first year alone he spent $150,000 of his own money, from an income estimated roughly at $250,000 a year.[4]

He had by that time sold many of his stocks, part of a general unloading of corporate responsibilities as he shifted from business into full-time politics. Alberta Pacific Grain he had sold to Spillers of England in 1924, Eddy's stock he had sold in 1928 to an international match consortium, and much of the rest of his holdings had probably been sold and reinvested more conservatively.

On his way through Winnipeg, probably early in 1929, he got Jack Haig, a local Conservative MLA, to drive him around. 'I'm selling all my stocks, Jack,' he said. 'Why,' Haig wanted to know. 'Well,' Bennett said, 'you sell yours, and in a few years from now I will tell you why.' Haig did not have to wait that long to find out.[5]

Bennett brought with him a well-established feud with the Siftons and their powerful paper the *Manitoba Free Press*, together with its adroit editor, John W. Dafoe. Bennett had early crossed Arthur Sifton, chief justice of the North-West Territories and then of Alberta from 1903 to 1910, for his politics, his law, and his flagrant hedonism. He liked Sir Clifford Sifton little better, or his son Victor, who dominated the eastern prairies with the *Free Press* and John W. Dafoe. Dafoe could be spiteful; his technique was to cleverly misrepresent his opponent's position and then proceed to demolish it. Dafoe regarded R.B. Bennett as a fraud, pompous and vain; R.B. thought of Dafoe as a Liberal hired gun, his editorials as outmoded as his clothes. Dafoe affected the rumpled tweedy look, as if he had been sleeping in his clothes for a week; Bennett liked his shoes shined, his trousers pressed. He liked to look the part he was called on to play, perhaps in principle not unlike Dafoe.[6] Like all appearances, both were deceptive.

R.B. loved to have fun at the expense of the Winnipeg *Free Press*. During the 1927 convention a young reporter approached him:

'Mr. Bennett, I represent the Free Press.'
'Yes, of course, the London Free Press.'
'Mr. Bennett, have you never heard of the Winnipeg Free Press?'
'Well, now, let me see.'
'Surely, Mr. Bennett, you have heard of Mr. Dafoe?'
'Dafoe? Oh, yes, of course! He is the man who wrote Robinson Crusoe.'[7]

He was an inveterate tease. When he knew that William Herridge, his brother-in-law, was in a desperate hurry about something, as likely as not he would find ways to delay it. One day Herridge got hold of Rod Finlayson, Bennett's private factotum, on the phone from Washington. Had he spoken to Bennett as Herridge had asked? 'Yes.' 'What's he doing about it?' 'Well,' said Finlayson, 'he's giving the matter some thought.' 'Oh, God pity us,' exclaimed Herridge, 'We'll never get anywhere as long as that stupid stubborn bastard is the head of the government.' The stupid stubborn bastard was listening, chuckling to himself, on the other office phone.[8]

Dr Robert Manion one day in cabinet began with, 'I was just thinking, Chief ...' R.B. looked at him icily. 'You were what, Bob?' Since Manion could return in kind, their relations were fairly harmonious. But with some other colleagues that ironic teasing did not always work. One day Finlayson was in the Rideau Club with Thomas Murphy, minister of the interior and member for Neepawa. Bennett was sitting nearby with Arthur Merriam, and said, not too *sotto voce*, 'Will you just look at those two great Manitoba statesmen in conference?' Both Merriam and Finlayson understood that sort of banter; Finlayson wondered if it might not have rankled with Murphy.[9]

R.B. enjoyment a good argument. If you wanted to win with him you ought not to be timid, but be quite ready to give as good as you got. He liked his answers straight from the shoulder. He had his enmities, though, which, once well established, were apt to become eternal. Neither he nor Dafoe were strong on the biblical injunction to forgive your enemies. That was New Testament, and Bennett was strong on the Old, on the prophets, with a penchant for Amos, Hosea, and Micah. There was not much about forgiveness in those books of the Bible, and a good deal about God's severity to his enemies.

R.B. found it hard to forgive Harry Stevens for jumping the

gun and publishing a pamphlet on price spreads before the publication of the royal commission's report, especially since Stevens was its chairman. The rest of the cabinet were just as angry, especially Cahan. Thus heavily criticized, Stevens resigned, his second resignation in ten months. This time, in October 1934, it was accepted. Two months after that, Stevens's seventeen-year-old daughter Sylvia died in Montreal after an operation. Arthur Merriam, Bennett's secretary,[10] suggested that it would be decent, even politic, if the chief would meet the train from Montreal as it was on its way through Ottawa to Vancouver, since Stevens was accompanying his daughter's body. So it would have been. R.B. would have none of it. Stevens's treachery still rankled. Herridge said of R.B., 'Isn't he an uncharitable bugger!' Bennett's memory was too lively, like a Scotsman's, and at some distance from charity.

Such established hates must be distinguished from R.B.'s short-fuse temper, which could be as ephemeral as passing showers, and sometimes as refreshing. A good example was a speech he made early in 1929 to the Macdonald-Cartier Club of Winnipeg. It was a gathering of the faithful, of Conservatives active and passive. Among them was a forty-three-year-old Winnipeg lawyer, Rod Finlayson, who, introduced to Bennett, told him he could not accept some of Bennett's ideas about the British Empire. R.B. eyed Finlayson curiously, wondering how he had got into the meeting, then in clipped accents said, 'If you want to get out of the British Empire, say so. No need for discussion.' Bennett's Winnipeg audience cared little about the Balfour Report of 1926; Bennett rather played to this and gave them what they liked; his pro-Empire oratory was enthusiastically received. The more Finlayson listened and the more he drank, the angrier he got. When asked to speak, therefore, he let himself go with a vengeance. Bennett's imperial policies were two generations behind the times, he said; he recalled sharply how Sir John Macdonald refused to bail out Gladstone and Company in 1884. The effect was electric, as if Finlayson had thrown a brick through a stained-glass window. He was booed furiously; his closest friends at his table refused to talk to him. He was leaving the meeting, alone, when R.B. sought him out, shook his hand warmly and said, 'Finlayson, I didn't agree with you, but you spoke well.' This was typical of Bennett. It was also typical that in 1931 he hired Finlayson as a private secretary. He would sometimes call up a young MP, often from the opposite side with whom he had crossed swords in the House of Commons, and congratulate him on his speech. Mackenzie King was not so generous.[11]

R.B. was exigent but generous to those who worked for him. On one occasion he and Alice Millar had set out by car towards Cochrane to give prizes at a small school. They couldn't find the entrance to the schoolyard and took a short cut through a barbed-wire fence. He held it up for her, then she for him; but she let go too soon and the barbed wire tore a large three-cornered rent in the Bennett overcoat. He was not pleased, and made some bitter remark about the frailty of humans! But fundamentally he was kind and Alice knew it. If he worked his staff hard, he would not order, but ask, 'Would you do ...?' He was jovial and polite with his secretaries, his chauffeur, his cook.[12]

He would fight with great determination for someone whom he thought was victimized by authority; when the Canadian Pacific Railway fired a conductor who had been giving passengers fares lower than the standard tariff Bennett got the man reinstated. However, he had no charity for real breaches of trust. What he believed is well summed up in his assessment of Chief Justice Francis Anglin of the Supreme Court of Canada, who died in March 1933. It suggests something of R.B.'s ideas about himself:

The principal factor in making possible the great success of Chief Justice Anglin was his ability to work and work and work ... the duty of man being to 'do justice, love mercy, and walk humbly with his God.' Justice is an attribute of a godhead, and it must always be tempered with mercy; and humility is the hall-mark of those who do justice and love mercy.[13]

R.B. was a shrewd judge of men, women, and character. When in 1917 D.L. Redman, a former law partner, became the member of Parliament for Calgary, he brought his handsome young wife Jean with him to Ottawa. She was a western girl, and came down east very uncertain of herself and her capacity socially. She asked Bennett for advice on behaviour at Ottawa functions. He told her she was just to continue to look beautiful and to keep her mouth shut. It worked.[14]

He had a perceptive eye for talent and recruited brilliantly for the public service of Canada. He brought Clifford Clark out of Queen's University in 1932 to be deputy minister of finance, a position he was to retain for the next twenty years. He appointed Lester Pearson, an unknown in External Affairs, as secretary of the Stevens Royal Commission on Price Spreads. O.D. Skelton, the Canadian nationalist who was deputy minister of external affairs, was kept on after 1930 despite Skelton's profound distrust of the British, simply for his judgment, his loyalty, and his experience. He brought Herbert McKinnon to National Revenue although his antecedents were Liberal party. Bennett appointed and promoted on the basis of ability; his passion for efficiency, his belief in a strong and talented civil service, was largely proof against political partisanship.

It was the same with honours and knighthoods. R.B. believed in them, and with him they were severely non-political. 'I never gave a political honour in my life,' he said proudly. The practice of recommending honours had been abandoned in 1919 on the basis of a resolution of the House of Commons. But that resolution had never been passed by the Senate; hence, in Bennett's view, it was invalid. His recommendations for New Year's Honours in

1934 included jurists, researchers, poets, musicians: Sir Lyman
Duff; Sir Frederick Banting, and Sir Charles Saunders; Sir Charles
G.D. Roberts, Sir Ernest MacMillan. Charlotte Whitton got her
CBE in 1934 along with five other well-known women. The OBEs
comprehended one man and fifteen women, among them Lucy
Maud Montgomery. Henry Wise Wood got a CMG in 1935. Not
a single member of R.B.'s cabinet got a knighthood, and he him-
self refused honours from Britain in 1932.[15]

R.B. has been accused more than once of running a one-man
government. It is true he liked quick, direct decisions. A good
example is an incident in August 1930, only a fortnight after his
government was sworn in. He and his sister Mildred were coming
through Lake Louise one Sunday and ran across an old friend,
Red Cooper. 'Well, Red,' said R.B., 'are you making a living?'
'Yes,' Red answered, 'but there are tens of thousands of poor
devils that cannot make it. You should do something for them
right now.' 'Yes, Red, and what can I do for them right now?'
Red replied, 'Let's build a road from here to Jasper.' Within ten
days, surveyors and men were out beginning work on the Banff-
Jasper highway. It was federal land, federal parks, and Bennett
acted.[16]

The truth was he could not bear inefficient or lazy ministers.
Arch Dale's wonderful cartoon of an R.B. Bennett cabinet is too
good: it is tremendous humour and a quarter truth. In R.B.'s first
session of 1931, it is true, he kept his eye on his ministers like a
schoolmaster watching his pupils perform before their parents.
This he measurably relaxed as time went on; he controlled his
cabinet by his power, energy, and talent. R.J. Manion explained
that R.B. was not a domineering prime minister: 'Most of us handled our departments without either his direction or his interfer-
ence.' The problem was that although in caucus he was often
content to sit in a corner and listen, he ignored his cabinet colleagues in his public utterances.[17] And he commanded the House
of Commons as Mackenzie King never could.

In 1938 Agnes Macphail, the CCF member for Grey-Bruce and the first woman elected to the Commons, thought R.B. was the most fascinating man in it. She was of the opinion that his sometimes dictatorial manner, and his relative failure to develop fully the capabilities of his party followers, was 'rooted in his great abilities. He can do each task so much more efficiently and with much less irritation if he does it himself; so he just does. He often reminds me of a very efficient mother, who, because she can do things so much better than her family, does all the work, to their detriment.' She thought he was much the most colourful character in the House.

He displays before our eyes the whole gamut of human emotions, according to his mood. In a happy mood, he teases and cajoles the House; again, he earnestly and forcefully builds a logical argument, and, where an impartial decision is needed, he can exhibit judicial qualities. But, when aroused, he can storm and rage as can none other.[18]

It has to be conceded, however, that Agnes Macphail, like Charlotte Whitton, was personally fond of R.B., some twenty years her senior. Their names had been associated in various ways. One widow wrote R.B. in 1933 that he must not marry Agnes Macphail because she herself had already marked him down for her second husband![19]

R.B. Bennett's relations with women, beginning with his mother, is a long and extraordinary story. Like King he was a bachelor, and like King, never a misogynist. One complaint in Parliament, when both were leaders of their parties, was that they had been bachelors so long that both had been spoiled by women. Had they been married, some of those idiosyncratic edges would have been sanded off. Bennett was fond of women, but he was shy, sentimental, and vulnerable. He seems not to have had much opportunity to collect social skills.

The influence of a strong, ambitious, and attractive mother, whose husband never satisfied her intellectual, social, and economic drives, is never to be underestimated, especially with eldest sons; it affected both King and Bennett powerfully, though in different ways. As Bennett said, 'My mother was such a guiding star.' He was writing to Alma Russell in 1914 after his return from his mother's funeral at Hopewell Cape. 'Life seems very dark and sad,' he went on, 'the shadows deepen. I am now travelling down the western slope of life but I shall not forget the girl I knew when life was young & hope was strong who has ever been indeed a true & sympathetic friend.'[20]

This elegiac tone – downhill on the western slope of life, when he was forty-four years of age – was, in fact, legitimate; but not many would have used it, or so expressed it. But even more surprising were his reflections on marriage, a decade earlier. Max Aitken wrote in July 1904 from Halifax to announce that he was engaged to be married, to Gladys Drury, a striking Halifax beauty and the daughter of Colonel Charles Drury, commander of the Halifax garrison. Max's pending marriage gave Dick Bennett to reflect about marriage and himself:

I am now almost an old man.[!] I will not marry. I guess I have made a mistake but it can't be remedied. May I say though that I think a woman to be a wife in the best and true sense of the term must while being domestic in her tastes have such large sympathies and mental qualities as to be able to enter into the ambitions & hopes of her husband whatever they may be.[21]

That is extraordinary considering that R.B. had just turned thirty-four – not exactly old even by 1904 standards. Beaverbrook offers the suggestion that R.B. feared he might be dominated by a wife, or brought to unhappiness by some clash of temperament. Even when in love, he would indicate that he would never marry.[22]

There may be more to it than R.B.'s fear of domination. His

age may in fact have had little to do with it. There is one suggestion, from a strange source, of what the difficulty might have been: the records of the Progressive Conservative party. This unlikely archive has a file on R.B. Bennett, written anonymously, but often accurate. At least the hypothesis is worth noting: his problem could have been medical. It was asserted he had phimosis, a tight foreskin, causing him to wince in pain at erection.[23] This condition, not uncommon, is easily remedied by surgery now, but in Dick Bennett's adolescence and early manhood it was not. Perhaps ultimately it was remedied, by the time of his most serious romance, in 1932. It would not have been difficult, for R.B. watched his health, and on his frequent visits to London consulted expert doctors. There are records of those examinations; none mention that condition.[24] On the other hand, that it was not mentioned would not be altogether surprising. The hypothesis does help explain what is otherwise not easily explicable. We have some idea of why Mackenzie King never married: he was too greedy. He wanted a lady who had money, beauty, charm, address, intelligence, who adored him, and who was available. He never found such a paragon. With R.B. the situation is different. As the party record explains, he had a reputation with women; he was tall, handsome, well turned out. But while his approach was frequently bold, he was fundamentally shy and nervous; his condition would only have made that shyness worse.

Thus R.B.'s long and remarkable intimacy with his sister becomes more understandable. No one can seriously suggest that there was anything improper in their long co-habitation in suites in the Palliser at Calgary, and Chateau Laurier in Ottawa. But some facts can be borne in mind. For instance, Mildred's arrival in the world, 26 March 1889, came as a distinct surprise to her forty-five-year-old mother; Mildred's birth came as an even greater, and pained, surprise to Dick Bennett, school-teaching in Douglastown on the Miramichi.[25] He got used to the idea, but he did not see much of his new sister except on periodic visits to Hopewell Cape, invariably at Christmas, sometimes in summer. So naturally Mildred grew up outside his immediate ken. There are one or two early letters, one from Mildred on her eighth birthday, announcing that it had been too stormy to have her birthday party.[26] Mildred went to Mount Allison University, her fees almost certainly paid by her Calgary brother, now doing very well. She returned home to help look after her mother, until Mrs Bennett died in 1914. Then Mildred went to Vancouver to stay with her sister Evelyn, fifteen years older, who had married a Vancouver minister, Dr H.W. Coates.

To Dick, Mildred became more a cousin than a sister, and a very attractive woman. From 1924 on Mildred would visit him at the Palliser, and by 1929 had come to live there en suite, occupying a place in his life that few sisters could or would have occupied. Dick was the most attractive and interesting man of her acquaintance. She was now an experienced and well-travelled woman of thirty-five, having been abroad several times with her brother on his business travels to London. She knew England better than she knew Canada, having never been west until she went to Vancouver. She was devoted to Dick, and he to her, in ways that strike one as remarkable. They admired, loved, each other. Mildred often used to say that 'she would be married on the same day her brother was, and not before.'[27] One day Mildred turned to Alice Millar, and said to her, 'Millar, don't ever walk out on Dick. We're the bumpers on his car. We save him a lot of damage.'[28]

Mildred had qualities her brother lacked. She loved a party; she could dance; she liked the odd glass of champagne; and she had that indefinable quality that men call charm – that is, tact, vivacity, a sense of humour, willingness to listen. To all this was joined great political sagacity. Rod Finlayson thought she had a better grasp of prevailing currents of opinion than either R.B. or Herridge.[29] She and R.B. both had large reserves of pity, but she deployed hers openly and splendidly, the way she did everything. In a New York hospital where she was an out-patient, she found herself amidst, as she put it, 'the old, the low and the high,' children hanging on to their mother's skirts, crying when their mother had to go for treatment. Mildred looked at them sadly and said to herself, 'What has Capitalism done for you?'[30] Mildred had the moral sweep of Shaw's Candida, superior to both the principal men of her life.

There was pity in R.B. too, but it was apt to be reined in by duty and responsibility, by his impatience over recklessness with money, and, even more, by disregard of ordinary honesty. Moral turpitude usually changed R.B.'s charity from grace into obligation. The best example is his relations with his brother George, the family ne'er-do-well. George had been a great disappointment to Dick for many years, before and after the Great War; he was too frequently drunk, invariably hard up, and would live most of his life dependent on his brother. One condition of R.B.'s support was that he live at Fort MacMurray, which he did most of the time, though he would make sudden and devastating raids on Edmonton and Calgary in search of money or drink. In the 1920s George had fathered an illegitimate child, Joan Bennett, whose education and upkeep also became R.B.'s responsibility. This fund was administered through a lawyer friend, and very much at arm's length. R.B. found it impossible to embrace the young girl who was the result of his brother's sin.[31]

R.B. could even get cross at Mildred when she wanted money for something he thought outrageous, though he was generous in his gifts to her. One day he encountered her in the Palliser sharing a bottle of champagne with an old friend. R.B. said they were both drunk and refused to speak to her for two days. Mildred understood R.B.'s temperament; she was really the only person who knew how to handle him. Like him, she never flinched from an argument, but she was the better mediator, and she would elicit political views from anyone, anywhere, of any party.[32]

Mildred was soon indispensable to R.B. and to the Conservative party. She really helped her brother win the 1930 election.[33]

When her engagement to William Herridge was announced, early in 1931, a *cri de coeur* arose from the ranks of the party. As one supporter in Ontario wrote, 'There is no position in the gift of the Conservative party that she has not earned and should not have if she chooses. Her departure will be an irreparable loss to you and the Conservative party.' One lady wrote to R.B., 'I think I know what you feel about her marriage. I never saw such love between a brother and a sister before.'34

Mildred and William Herridge were married in Ottawa on 14 April 1931. Mildred seems to have been somewhat disconcerted by the change in her mode of life. The most remarkable of her letters was the note she wrote Dick as she was packing up in the suite of the Chateau Laurier, where she and her brother had lived for four years:

Dick, my dear dear brother,

I can't leave this address without a little note to you – If I could only say all that is in my heart but I can't – and I know that you realize that in the midst of my most sacred and divine love you have never for moment been out of my mind – In fact, I sometimes wonder if I am not going to be very lonely for you. I've *not* changed and never will. I sometimes think that loving Bill as I do – I've loved and valued you even more –

I can't write more my darling Dick, but always my adoration and devotion to the grandest and finest brother a sister ever had –

> Ever and *forever*,
> Your devoted sister,
> Mildred,35

After Mildred had gone to live in Washington with her husband, R.B. seems to have become more sharply aware of the great domestic vacancy in his life, that huge interior space, that Mildred left. Frank Regan, of CNR hotels, wrote him the day after Mildred's wedding, 'I think of you in your loneliness and you have my sympathy and understanding.' R.B. was fully aware of what Mildred had meant to him, personally and politically.[36]

Then a year later, in the spring of 1932, a lady came into R.B.'s life – newly widowed, attractive, intelligent, wealthy, and well imbued with Conservative politics. Hazel Beatrice Kemp Colville was born the same year as Mildred, in 1889, but in very different circumstances. She was the daughter of a wealthy Toronto Conservative, Sir Edward Kemp, a Methodist millionaire who had made his money in graniteware, and who lived on Castle Frank Crescent, Rosedale. Her daughter remembers her mother claiming to be the first woman in Toronto with a driver's licence! In 1911 Hazel married Francis Stephens. A daughter, Frances, was born on 15 September 1912. When the war broke out Stephens went overseas; he got trench fever in France, was invalided back to Canada, and died in the influenza epidemic of the autumn of 1918.[37]

Hazel Kemp Stephens was now a thirty-year-old widow with an eight-year-old daughter. She was not poor; her father was wealthy and her husband had left her well provided for. She was a woman of great spirit and energy; she was also one of those women to whom men are attracted like moths to light. She put forth no arts and no tricks; she just was what she was. In January 1920 she married a well-to-do lawyer, Arthur Colville, a war veteran like her first husband. Colville used to say the only things a gentleman should be seen carrying were wine and cigarettes; the latter were his undoing. He liked strong Egyptian cigarettes, and smoked heavily. Noticeably unwell in 1929, he developed cancer of the throat and died in May 1931 at the age of forty-four.[38] Widowed a second time, Hazel Kemp Colville, now very well off indeed, bought and restored the manor house of Pierre le Gardeur de Repentigny at Mascouche, northeast of Montreal, just north of Rivière des Prairies. She published an elegant little pamphlet of its history.[39]

Hazel Colville had known R.B. through her father, Sir Edward Kemp. Kemp had served in the Borden government since 1911, becoming minister of militia and defence after Sir Sam Hughes was fired in November 1916. Kemp and R.B. were briefly cabinet colleagues in Meighen's 1920–1 government, after Bennett joined it as minister of justice in October 1921. Hazel thought she knew him well enough to call him 'R.B.,' as she reminded him when she wrote him in January 1930, asking a series of policy questions about immigration.[40]

The acquaintanceship so renewed developed rapidly. There were certainly men in her life before R.B. came along. But by the summer of 1932, when the Ottawa Imperial Conference was in full swing, he found solace, comfort, and delight in the company of Hazel Colville. She was instrumental in helping to rescue him from the toil and turmoil of those hectic weeks of late July and August 1932. After the conference broke up on Saturday, 20 August, R.B. went over to Mascouche for four days to recover. He returned to Ottawa for a civic reception, and although he went through the motions, answering questions, talking to friends, all he could think of was Hazel Colville. The letters begin Saturday, 27 August 1932, and they open with R.B. already in love:

> Chateau Laurier
> Ottawa
> Canada
> Saturday

Beloved,

All day yesterday, a day of great contrasts and amazing experiences, you were with me. The city address was quite too trying at 11. Somehow it shook the very foundations of my being and I am afraid it was not because of the reasons assigned by the Mail & Empire today, but because just before I replied that dear face was so clear & near beside me, just over the right shoulder but with tears in her eyes: It was quite too real for words ...[41]

That evening in a speech he even talked of wanting to give up political life. The next day he would be on his way to Calgary, with Mildred (up from Washington) and Alice Millar:

I shall think tonight as I journey west of a week ago & the sunlight ... And I will be sad & pity myself & be thankful that I know you & grateful for all you have meant to me. As the day ends of the drive in [to Hawkesbury] & the memories will crowd upon me & I will be both sad & happy. I wonder if you can understand? I have just rec'd word of the desire of Calgary to have a reception for me. And that will di-vert[?] me with the thought ... that you should come too!! Be a real pal & write me a line to the Palliser Hotel, Calgary. It would so please me to see your handwriting & have a few words from you: And I am not too hard to please & make happy you know ... I hear that Toronto has quite a series of stories about you & I. Mildred says Lady Kemp she saw yesterday: She is ciphering out the relationship of a step-mother to a stepdaughter's husband!! I must close this note which I may *not* mail. We will see: But I miss you beyond all words & I am lonesome beyond cure without your presence [?] & oo I go with all my love,

Ever your grateful & devoted old man,

[PS] I am going to mail this without waiting – Oh my dear how I miss you. I really am just a poor weak emotional man, hungry for a sight of you ...[42]

On the train westward, R.B. watched Lake Superior roll by, think-ing of Hazel and of the changes time had wrought in the few past weeks. He was writing on the jolting train:

I am *not* content to just accept a mere casual disposition of what is so important. After all we do know one another very very well & it is not fitting that we should end our relations in just casual forgetfulness: For I cannot & will not forget: You are quite part of the greatest days of my life and one of the greater events in the life of the dominion:43 So you first [?] think it over carefully, won't you dear? I recall your query 'am I asleep or dreaming?' You have been doing neither ... How I have recalled the last 4 days: The first seems so very long ego: I went to Hawkesbury but it might have been another life ... It meant so much to me – Mildred has been teasing me all day ... It is still like a real physical pain in my left side: There is no *reason* for it. By all the rules it should not be & yet, it is ... You will forgive me dearest if I suggest fewer cigarettes per day: You do smoke too much: And I only say it because your health is so important to us all. Hope you can read this letter as the train rocks so hard: The white haired head & the beloved face I have seen in all my waking hours. And do not think me silly for saying so. How I wish I could be with you. But that cannot be & I will with all my love & devotion sign myself ever your loving old man.

R.B.44

Back in Ottawa in mid-September, he was again at Mascouche on weekends. He was happier than he had ever been; he enclosed a proof (a ring or bracelet, perhaps?) of his deep and abiding affection 'which is beyond words: But let me cling in happiness to my beloved word "absolutely; & with all my devotion & affection subscribe myself in truth ever & forever your own old man, R.B."'45

The new parliamentary session at Ottawa would open Thursday, 6 October 1932. After that, he said, 'I suppose I am tied to the oar as the galley slave of old. *But* I hope I can go out to the Manoir on Sunday the 9th!! Probably it will be the last visit I can make this coming month.' He did got to Mascouche that weekend, Thanksgiving, and gave thanks for it:

It was & is of course the charm of the seigneuresse: What a delightful
hostess, what a kind & thoughtful friend: But oh! what a glorious
sweetheart! (Dare I write that) How I did enjoy the walk through the
woods. It was wonderful – But the wonder really was that I had as
guide *you* ...

But most of all on this day I render thanks for you & all dear heart
you are to me with the hope that every Thanksgiving Day of this
mortal life may find me having the same sentiments & thankfulness
but stronger with the lapse of years – God bless & keep you my dear
& may I sign with devotion & affection, ever yours in truth & fact.

R.B.[46]

A week later he was in Toronto at Sunday service in Hazel's
old church, Sherbourne Street United, and read the memorial to
her parents on the wall. He visited her sisters in Rosedale. R.B.
was amused at the last observation of Hazel's sister when he left,
the family joke (already) that Hazel Colville was to be new senator
of Repentigny! The sister added, 'Unless she aspires to something
higher!' R.B. remarked, 'I cannot say about the aspirations but I
can say about the opportunity she has!!' His seven-page letter to
Hazel went on:

Life is a strange thing. We cannot determine by any action we may
take what the results of such a given action will be: Think of all that
has happened since April. It cannot be explained on any reasonable
ground. *But it has happened* ... A new aspect to life; a new view of the
future; a happiness made greater by its unhappiness, if that can be
understood. 'The wind bloweth where it listeth' None can explain
why the heart turns to that of another: For me to repeat that I am
glad beyond measure words that the change has come to me even so
late in life as it has ...[47]

He was at Mascouche again the weekend of 29–30 October:

I shall never forget the last Sunday of October 1932 ... I cannot tell
you the effect of that letter. Never have I read a more moving communication – I was right in what I told you yesterday. I do & should
feel badly. But I will not fail you. I wish you had just sent it to me
before. And now that I know all the terrible struggle why of course I
will show to you that I can be of use & that my will [?] is not a total
failure: But dearest do not get into the awful habit of being introspec-
tive. It is no good & will just ruin you. There is no need of resorting
to heroic measures. Your old man will not be unworthy of your trust
... Such a letter: How it has moved me. How often I have I read it.
Nothing dear that you have ever said or done has quite so touched
me. It is quite beyond words. And I know that in the morrow [?] you
will be just what your great faith dictates & that peace will follow &
we will keep it.[48]

He was still thinking about it all the next day:

It has meant so much to me to be able to go down to your place on
the weekend: What delightful anticipation & of joyous realization –
Care has dropped from me as a mantle discarded ... I shall ever hold
that deep & indescribable devotion for you that so strangely has come
upon me at this late hour of life: And it has all been good for me:
Sweetened my views of life & people & made me a much happier
person even tho' I do find it irksome to be so held in leash by the
party I lead – It is not only unfair but I cannot permit it to continue
much longer. I will not write longer: This is in the nature of a 'peace
offering.' I am so happy when I am at the Manor House & with
you ...[49]

R.B. and Hazel took care to avoid publicity about their friendship. His car would take him to some rendezvous point – Hawkesbury turns up in letters often – and her car would meet him
there and he would be whisked off to Mascouche.[50] But since he
was at Mascouche almost every second weekend, from August

to November, Canada's prime minister could not escape. It was in the papers over the weekend of 22–23 October 1932 that romance, even marriage, was in train. The rumours were not so much denied as resented. Bennett sent a telegram to J.W. Reardon, editor of the *Boston Advertiser*, which would carry the news in its Sunday edition. The current issue 'is greatly resented by reason of its unchivalrous & false article.' The editor apologized, said he had been misled by a Canadian correspondent and the *Toronto Star*.[51] R.B. was chivalrously annoyed, but was not altogether uncharmed by the idea. The old politicians around Ottawa, he wrote Hazel, were worried, very worried 'about their leader!! Is he in great danger from a "designing woman"?'[52]

He tried also to charm Hazel's daughter Frances, in his avuncular way, for he was fond of her. She found him a bit awkward to meet and talk to, wordy, almost too articulate and formal, as if, at least with a twenty-year-old, he could not quite unbend, or shed his old role as school master. When he would come to call at 1371 Pine Avenue in Montreal, however, her mother would usually ask her, 'Couldn't you go somewhere?'[53]

Hazel Colville worried about those love letters from R.B. On 24 November 1932 she took all her letters from him, sealed them, and handed them to the Royal Trust, Montreal. On the wrapping was written: 'Not to be opened by anyone. Can be given to my daughter in 1950 if not destroyed by me before that date.' They never were destroyed.

R.B. left for England early in December 1932, still a bachelor despite the rumours, duly noted by the *Ottawa Journal*.[54] Then in March 1933 Hazel went abroad for a couple of months and the rumours subsided. The correspondence suggests, not that R.B.'s ardour had cooled, but that Hazel had become unwell; she also seems to have wanted more space in their relations.

Bennett was busy; he was again in England in the summer of 1933 with the World Economic Conference that opened in South Kensington on 12 June. He continued to write to Hazel and get cables and letters about her health. Lady Londonderry, companion to the British prime minister, Ramsay MacDonald, referred to R.B. as Canada's strongman. The strong man was amused. ' "Strong man"!' he wrote Hazel, 'You know what a misnomer that is don't you? I am able quietly to do considerable in the way of directing the channels of thought: That is not egotism & Don't you think so!'[55] He worried about her health and her playing too much tennis and golf and smoking too much. And he wanted her letters. He was going up to Harrogate for a rest cure when the conference was over and added: 'Please do not leave me all alone!! Ever your devoted Dick.'[56]

There are only two more letters. One is a single word, written on 21 September 1933: 'No! Dick.' The last was penned on his way to New Brunswick for Christmas 1933, written from the train and on a rough track.[57] It was going to get rougher.

Hazel Colville was not the sort of woman who could be persuaded to do anything against her will. She had always charted her own course. She did not need men; they needed her. She liked her bridge and cigarettes, and doubtless drinks. Sometime early in 1934 R.B. came to call on Hazel at her Montreal house. What exactly happened is not known, for her daughter Frances was not there. Whatever did occur, R.B. left so angry that he stalked out, leaving his cane behind. He never came back for it. It is still there, so to speak, in 1992. Hazel's daughter has it in Oakville: a stout, knobbly blackthorn, the thorns cut neatly off, a series of half-inch rounds, reminders, perhaps, of prickliness gone. Around the top of the cane is a heavy gold band on which is printed: 'Richard Bedford Bennett, July 3, 1930.'[58] It was a gift for his sixtieth birthday, perhaps from Mildred.

Hazel and R.B. in 1934 went their separate ways.[59] Colville family tradition had it that R.B. went to England in 1938–9 partly as a reaction to that failed love affair. Whatever the truth of that, it is virtually certain that R.B. would have married Hazel Colville had she been willing. Beaverbrook thought so, and regretted that it never happened. So did R.B. There was that poem he sent to

Hazel in September 1932, asking her to read it and destroy it –
a poem that may well have symbolized her thinking and presaged
the end of their late-season romance:

> In truth we might have known it from the start,
> This path would have its turning; there would be
> No real alternative for you and me,
> Fashioned of honest earth, except to part.
> Whether the blow were mine to deal, or whether
> Yours the swift blade by which this bond were sundered,
> The hearts must bleed, because the feet have blundered
> Into a way we may not walk together.
>
> Rebuke me not, beloved, in that I
> Perforce do quickly that which needs must be
> I am as one who fights because she fears
> A darker wound, a deadlier agony
> Than fronts her now. And if I say good-bye
> Believe me that I say it through my tears![60]

What might have happened had R.B. married? Pure, and useless, speculation, perhaps. But was it possible that R.B. was right
when he wrote to Hazel, that All Saints Day in 1932, that his
devotion to her, that had come so strongly and strangely upon
him so late in his life, had made him a happier person? Had it,
as he said, 'sweetened my views of life and people'? Perhaps the
Toronto Star was right, anti-Bennett though it was, when in January 1933 it found R.B. more likeable, more human, more reasonable, 'more winning, in a word.'[61]

By 1933 R.B. was facing what he felt was the greatest crisis in
Canada's history. He wrote to Sir Robert Borden in October 1933:

The real difficulty is that we are subject to the play of forces which
we did not create and which we cannot either regulate or control. We

are between the upper and the nether millstone. We are a debtor country, and a debtor country must suffer under the conditions with which we are threatened. Our people have been very steady, but they are depressed and, having listened on the radio to so much 'ballyhoo', they are now demanding Action! Action!! Action!!! Any action at this time except to maintain the ship of state on an even keel and trim our sails to benefit by every passing breeze involves possible consequences about which I hesitate even to think.[62]

Keeping the ship on an even keel was illustrated in Bennett's legislation of 1932 and 1933; action! action!! would follow in 1934 and 1935. Little of it was the result of sudden conversion. It was, rather, the result of decades of Borden-Bennett political philosophy: how the Canadian state could and should act, within its constitutional limits. R.B.'s long interest in government boards for regulating railway rates and public corporations, his support for government railways, his belief in workmen's compensation, unemployment insurance, labour unions – all these suggest a perspective different from the usual one of Bennett, the unredeemed capitalist, with dollar signs on his striped trousers and black coat. His appearance was the greatest illusion of all. He looked confident, master of all he surveyed; as the letters to Hazel Colville reveal, he was vulnerable, 'a poor, weak emotional man.' Those weaknesses he had conquered by a great self-discipline; his Wesleyanism had given him his exemplary determination, the triumph of his will over weaknesses of the self.

R.B. thought of himself as a reformer. When Rod Finlayson showed him suggestions for the January 1935 speeches, he said, 'Of course, I'm a reformer,' and reached for the *Hansard* of 1911 to prove it.[63] But as in 1911, he had not always been able to carry his party with him. Party differences could be borne when in opposition; but in office the party's right wing was more formidable. What really happened in 1932–5 was that the wing was finally brought, reluctantly, by the exigencies of the times, to accept what Bennett had long believed in.

Some of the great legislation of 1932–5 was also owing to legal decisions made at the Judicial Committee of the Privy Council in London. Bennett was too good a lawyer not to read with intense interest those words of Lord Sankey's in the *Aeronautics* case in 1932:

But while the Courts should be jealous in upholding the charter of the Provinces as enacted in section 92 it must no less be borne in mind that the real object of the [BNA] Act was to give the central Government those high functions and almost sovereign powers by which uniformity of legislation might be secured on all questions which were of common concern to all the Provinces.[64]

The *Radio* case, though decided on somewhat different grounds, gave Bennett's government early in 1932 the constitutional buttresses it needed for specific legislation. The Canadian Radio Communication Act was introduced by R.B. and went through the Commons with rare harmony; but that masked a great desire by politicians, on both sides of the House, to use government radio for their own purposes. R.B. was thinking of the BBC and got his way; he was not going to have the Canadian Radio Commission emasculated by its opponents in or outside of Canada.[65]

In the summer of 1933 R.B. appointed the Lord Macmillan Royal Commission to examine the possibility of establishing a Bank of Canada. It reported at the end of September, so recommending. The Canadian chartered banks did not like it; they had to give up their issue of currency, and, especially, they were required to transfer their gold reserves to the Bank of Canada. They would be paid for the gold, of course; the question was, at what price? If at the cost to them, it was $20.65 an ounce; if at the current market price, it was $35.40. R.B. was sure the act itself was constitutional, and he thought it was iniquitous that the chartered banks should try to make a 75 per cent capital gain at the expense of Canadian taxpayers. Dr G.D. Stanley was in Ottawa in May 1934 to see R.B. at the Chateau Laurier. R.B. had just come from meeting the general managers of the banks on that very subject. 'I never saw him,' remarked Stanley, 'so worked up and wrathy, almost vicious ...' One of his officials, James Stitt, went to him with the same question, could R.B. fight all the banks? R.B. replied, 'Jimmie Stitt, you quit worrying. We are going to get that gold and it is just about time for us to find out whether the banks or this government is running the country.' In the end he won. R.B. always regarded the creation of the Bank of Canada as his greatest domestic achievement.[66]

The best example of R.B. as an authentic radical was the Farmers' Creditors Arrangement Act of 1934. Despite his general belief that Canadians should pay legal obligations, live up to contracts, R.B. knew prairie life too well to stick at such points when dealing with the hardships of Saskatchewan and Alberta in the early thirties. He knew bankruptcy legislation, designed to give a fresh start to industrial enterprises; it was natural to apply the same principle to drought-stricken, mortgage-ridden farms and farmers. The act was designed to allow families to stay on the farms rather than lose them to foreclosure.[67]

Even more dramatic was the Prairie Farm Rehabilitation Act of 1935, which was in some ways the most remarkable of all of the Bennett legislation. It was a mighty enterprise, in effect an organization that would teach one hundred thousand farmers how to farm, how to rehabilitate the dust bowl.[68]

Thus the Bennett 'New Deal' was not all that new; much basic legislation was already in place. What was new was the Employment and Social Insurance Act, the 1935 centrepiece. It had long been considered by Bennett; what had held it up was constitutional doubts (now, since 1932, largely dissipated) and resistance in the Conservative party. Sir Lyman Duff, whom R.B. had appointed chief justice of Canada in 1933 and knighted in 1934, told Rod Finlayson that 'Bennett had ruined the Tory party with his damned New Deal.'[69] What was new in 1935, apart from unemployment insurance, was mostly Herridge's rhetoric, imported from Washington. Herridge and Finlayson wrote the speeches, Bennett delivered them.

While R.B. was out on speaking engagements in February 1935 he came down with a heavy cold, and then fibrillation of the heart was diagnosed. He was in bed for a month, then went to London to consult doctors and take in what he could of the Silver Jubilee. The doctors in Ottawa and London had electro-cardiagrams which showed 'paroxysmal auricular fibrillation.' One can still see R.B.'s heart condition in the tracings of the heartbeat. The doctors recommended easing back.[70] R.B. seriously considered it; he had thought indeed of retiring to England. But now there was the defection of Harry Stevens.

It was Stevens who made it impossible for Bennett to retire when all the medical evidence suggested he should. R.B. was *not* going to give up in the face of Stevens and a pending election! Mildred came north in June to help. There would be no surrender if she had anything to do with it! If R.B. was to go down to defeat it would be with all flags flying, full in the face of the enemy. 'I love Dick so much,' Mildred added, 'that often I long to see him defeated but ... we must put Canada first.' So she told Lord Beaverbrook. In the end, as everyone knows, R.B. lost the 1935 election. 'One man has crucified the Party,' R.B. told an old Calgary friend just before election day: 'Stevens.'[71]

Judged by popular vote, Bennett's defeat in October 1935 was not a massive one: the Conservatives took 30 per cent of the popular vote, the Liberals 45 per cent, and Stevens's Reconstruction Party and the CCF each about 8 per cent. But the effect in seats was devastating: Conservatives forty; Liberals 173; Reconstruction one; CCF seven; Social Credit seventeen.[72]

R.B. did not yet think of resigning. But by 1937 he was convinced he could no longer afford to lead the party; they seemed to expect him to provide money for everything. He was bitter over the way his 1927 convention resolution for the preservation of Sir John A. Macdonald's grave had been fudged and smudged by the Conservative member for Kingston, Brigadier-General A.E. Ross. The result was the new Liberal government rescued the grave and got all the credit. R.B. was bitter. 'I do not know anything that has impressed me more with the ingratitude of public life than the way this matter has been dealt with.' He wrote Ross with some anger, 'I am not unaware of my own limitations. I have made many mistakes, but I served this country as disinterestedly as any man who ever occupied public office, and I have never expected more than loyalty ... That I did not receive it may perhaps be a criticism of myself.'[73] That was his state of mind on resigning the leadership of the party in March 1938.

The hardest blow was yet to come. Mildred was the one person in the world R.B. loved more than anyone. She had been a delightful companion in the summer of 1937 when they had both gone to a German spa in Bad Neuheim. On her return she insisted she would improve and would soon be back to life with R.B. once more. 'I so often find myself thinking of the happy time we [you and I] had abroad ... Cheer up dear old brother of mine – we will make you Prime Minister again ...' She was in hospital in New York a few months later and R.B. visited her there. She loved him, loved his visit: 'How much good it did me to see my dear old brother who has always gone ahead of me and scattered roses in my path.'[74] R.B. returned to Ottawa convinced she was getting better. On the evening of Wednesday, 11 May 1938 at the Chateau he got the news of her sudden death. She was only forty-nine years old.

R.B. was shaken to the core. He shut himself up in her old room, pent up with grief, wordlessly pacing, then reading aloud to himself the book of Ruth. It was as if Ruth's devotion symbolized all the loyalty that had been his with Mildred: 'And Ruth said, Intreat me not to leave thee, or to return from following after thee: for whither thou goest, I will go ... [n]ought but death part thee and me.'

That night Arthur Meighen wrote R.B. from the Senate,

You have suffered today one of those devastating blows that aim to shatter one's hold on life. To a man of deep feelings and deep affections the impact comes all the harder. Many a time I thought how fortunate you were to have a sister of such charm, such intelligence and good sense, all accompanied by such unshakeable devotion to her brother.

O.D. Skelton wrote, 'It is only once in a generation that the world is blessed with a woman of such perfection of charm and kindliness and understanding.' It was hard to believe that the gay, splendid Mildred had gone, that 'the bright sunshine of her presence' – Alan Lascelles's words from Buckingham Palace – would be felt no more.[75]

A party convention in July 1938 elected R.J. Manion leader of the Conservative party. There was talk R.B. wanted to be asked to stay on, but there is little evidence for it. He went to England, took over Beaverbrook's contract to buy Juniper Hill, a sixty-acre estate next door to Max's at Cherkley. He then returned to Canada to wind up his affairs. He had had many offers to go into business, even to be a university president; but he felt he had been too long in the political arena to be considered neutral or dispassionate.[76]

He sailed from Saint John, New Brunswick, in the Canadian Pacific steamer *Montclare* late in January 1939. His last touch with Canadian soil had to be New Brunswick. When Halifax wanted to give him a reception he would not go ashore, so a large luncheon was arranged on board ship in Halifax harbour. It was a crowded, emotional affair; Bennett was in tears at the end of it. He resigned his seat as MP for Calgary that day. *Montclare* sailed for Liverpool that evening.

R.B. was made a viscount on 15 June 1941, taking the title Viscount Bennett of Mickleham, Calgary, and Hopewell. He had not anticipated the war, of course, and in many ways it played havoc with what he might have anticipated his life in England to be. Before leaving Canada in 1938 he had claimed to be a happy man, not lonely, too busy for loneliness. His was not a lonely nature, said Alice Millar.[77] But time and distance from Canada and those sixty acres that surrounded him at Juniper Hill had their own effects. He returned to Canada on a brief visit in 1941. John Stevenson remembered him at Shediac, sentimental and sad. 'It may not be a good thing,' he told Stevenson, 'to tear up one's roots as I have done.' R.B. looked out over the Shediac River, the islands, and the low, wooded hills around. 'I've spent the happiest summers of my boyhood here in New Brunswick. I've got my heart here. I love it with all my soul. All I have asked to do is to serve the land in which I was born.'[78]

In Mickleham, though, he had Max, and Alice Millar, and a devoted household staff. He was also well liked in the little village. He was a good squire. He had spent a good deal of money fixing up the house, putting in those Canadian requirements, central heating and modernized plumbing; he also put a small movie theatre in the basement. As the war came on he got into the habit of inviting the villagers over to Juniper Hill on Saturday nights to watch movies he had brought down from London. Refreshments would be offered. He grew to be liked and appreciated. He went to St George's, the local Anglican church, became a local justice of the peace.

On Thursday, 26 June 1947 he went up to London, as he often did on his multifarious business. It was hot. He came back in the afternoon and walked in the grounds with his dog Bill. Max came to call with two friends. R.B. was depressed, even despondent, and Max wanted him to come over to Cherkley for dinner. But R.B. dined alone. That evening at 10:30 he took a hot bath – he loved to soak in them – and died quietly there of a heart attack. He was still there in the morning when the butler came. The water had run over. The dog Bill was still asleep on the bed,[79] the last betrayal. He was buried in St George's churchyard, and the whole village turned out for the funeral.

The pub in Mickleham has been in existence since the eighteenth century and is called the *Running Horses*, after Epson Downs not far away. Some forty years after R.B. was buried a young Canadian showed up for ale in the public bar. His Canadian accent caught the ear of the publican. After a while the publican revealed that as a boy growing up in Mickleham he had known R.B. Bennett. He said to the young Canadian, Jeffrey Simpson, 'What on earth did you Canadians do to R.B. Bennett? You seem to have forced him out, almost as if you wanted to drive him into exile. Why? He was the nicest man imaginable.'[80] His brusqueness was, as *Saturday Night* observed,

the protective mask worn by a man who was essentially shy, essentially sentimental and essentially lonely for those closer relationships which an active lifetime had left no time to cultivate. That he did not exactly know how to play and that his attempt to do so led to an undeserved reputation for clumsiness of humour that was often mistaken for severity and heaviness ... But history will undoubtedly pay R.B. Bennett the tribute of having shielded the Dominion from the full effects of the worst economic storm the world has ever seen.[81]

So far, history hasn't.

Illustration Credits

Notes

INTRODUCTION

1 Norman Ward, ed., *A Party Politician, the Memoirs of Chubby Power* (Toronto 1966), 288
2 House of Lords Record Office, Beaverbrook Papers G/19, file XXVIII, Alice Millar to Beaverbrook, n.d., 1957, from St Lawrence Hotel, Barbados
3 University of New Brunswick Archives, R.B. Bennett Papers (hereafter RBB Papers), vol. 895, 560076, Alice Millar to Ronald V. Bennett, 6 August 1947, from Mickleham, Surrey
4 Interview with Professor A.G. Bailey, 17 June 1988, at UNB 'She threw away masses of material.' He complained to Beaverbrook about it, who replied that she was trying to protect Bennett's memory.
5 Lord Beaverbrook, *Friends: Sixty Years of Intimate Personal Relations with Richard Bedford Bennett* (London 1959)

1 HOPEWELL CAPE AND THE MIRAMICHI

1 See Esther Clark Wright, *The Petitcodiac* (Sackville, NB 1952), for a description of the remarkable river and its environment.
2 Ibid., 2. Esther Clark Wright was the daughter of Marriet Richardson Clark, who had lived at Hopewell Cape and was the friend of R.B. Bennett's sister Evelyn.

3 Charles G.D. Roberts, *The Heart that Knows* (New York 1906); reprinted, Sackville, NB 1984, 1

4 Harold Porter, 'Diary of my grandfather, Owen Porter,' ms. in possession of Jim Bennet, of Indian Harbour, Nova Scotia, 145–6. Owen Porter farmed in King's County, some thirty miles from Hopewell Cape.

5 Bliss Carman in 'Arnold, Master of the Scud,' in *Ballads and Lyrics* (Toronto 1923), 160

6 Census of Canada, 1870–1, I: 226; see the useful thesis by Donald Warren Smith, 'The Maritime Years of R.B. Bennett' (MA thesis, University of New Brunswick 1968). There is a typescript story of Albert County in the New Brunswick Museum, Saint John, W.C. Miller Papers, Box 1.

7 The first lines of 'Arnold, Master of the Scud.' See Malcolm Ross's excellent essay on Bliss Carman, 'Bliss Carman and the Poetry of Mystery: A Defence of the Personal Fallacy,' in Malcolm Ross, *The Impossible Sum of Our Traditions: Reflections on Canadian Literature* (Toronto 1986), 43–66.

8 RBB Papers, vol. 874, 543181 *et seq.*, have considerable material on the history of the Bennett family.

9 National Archives of Canada (NAC), MG28, IV-2 Progressive Conservative Party Records, Bennett file. Biographical note, not very friendly, but plausible, and in respect of Bennett's relations with the E.B. Eddy Co., accurate.

10 RBB Papers, vol. 875, 543794, Alma Russell to Alice Millar, 12 November 1948, from Victoria. This letter is Alma Russell's reminiscences, written in pencil.

11 Saint John Museum, Alma Russell Papers, R.B. Bennett to Alma Russell in Victoria, 1 November 1914, from Calgary. The letter is undated except marked 'Sunday'; the postmarked envelope gives the date. Bennett had just returned from New Brunswick, where his mother died on 1 October 1914. These letters were brought to my attention through the kindness of the archivists at the New Brunswick Museum.

12 RBB Papers, vol. 875, 543949. This is the reminiscence of a Miss or Mrs Read, a family friend in Hopewell Cape, solicited by Alice Millar. Miss Millar wrote on 29 June 1948, and the undated letter is in reply.

13 Census of Canada, 1881, District 23, Sub-District Cape Hopewell Division No. 1.

14 Wesley's famous sermon, 'The Use of Money,' was set down in this form in 1763, but it had a long gestation, in the form of comments and sermons on Luke, chapter 16, verse 9. See A.C. Outler, ed., *The Works of John Wesley* (Nashville 1985), II: 279, 273.

15 Ibid., 274 *et seq.*

16 See Goldwin French, *Parsons and Politics* (Toronto 1962), and more recently John Webster Grant, *A Profusion of Spires: Religion in Nineteenth Century Ontario* (Toronto 1988), 29–30, 58–9, 90–4, 138–41.

17 Robert C. Monk, *John Wesley, His Puritan Heritage* (London 1966), 215; also John Wesley, *The Works of the Reverend John Wesley*, ed. T. Jackson (London 1829), VIII: 345

18 Sermon No. 51, in *Works*, II: 295

19 So alleged Beaverbrook, in *Friends*, 6. Bennett's gifts and charities would eventually run to about 10 per cent of his gross income. His first gift to Dalhousie, his alma mater, in 1912, was $1,000, and he said it would have been more had he not to meet pressing demands from educational institutions in Calgary (Dalhousie University Archives (DUA), MS-1-3, A-148, Bennett to Dean R.C. Weldon, 10 June [1912], telegram, from Calgary). His charity in the 1930s is well known: see L.M. Grayson and M. Bliss, *The Wretched of Canada: Letters to R.B. Bennett, 1930–1935* (Toronto 1971).

20 RBB Papers, vol. 875, 543820, the reminiscences of Miss Annie Morrison of Douglastown, New Brunswick, 1948. She was in grade eight when Bennett taught her at Douglastown from 1888 to 1890.

21 Ernest Watkins, *R.B. Bennett* (Toronto 1963), 19–20

22 RBB Papers, vol. 876, 544205, report of provincial examinations at Fredericton, December 1886

23 Ibid., 544208, report of term ending 30 June 1887, at Irishtown, Parish of Moncton

24 ibid., vol. 875, 543794 *et seq.*, Alma Russell to Alice Millar, 12 November 1948

25 *Annual Report of Schools of New Brunswick, 1889*, report of RBB's

speech at the thirteenth annual meeting of the Northumberland County Teachers Institute; see also Donald Warren Smith, 'The Maritime Years of R.B. Bennett, 1870–1897' (MA thesis, University of New Brunswick 1965) 78–9; Ottawa *Morning Journal*, 21 May 1932; RBB Papers, vol. 876, 544148.

26 RBB Papers, vol. 875, 543820, recollections of Miss Annie Morrison
27 Ottawa *Morning Journal*, 21 May 1932
28 RBB Papers, vol. 875, 543794, Alma Russell to Alice Millar, 12 November 1948
29 *Chatham World*, 16 January 1889; RBB Papers, vol. 875, 543820, Mrs Louise Manny to Alice Millar, n.d.
30 RBB Papers, vol. 875, 543794, Alma Russell to Alice Millar, 12 November 1948
31 Beaverbrook, *Friends*, 6
32 House of Lords Record Office, Lord Beaverbrook Papers, G/39, Harold Girvan to Lady Dunn, 19 April 1956, from Victoria
33 RBB Papers, vol. 876, 544323, Diary, April 1890; July 1890; *Calendar of Dalhousie College and University, 1890–1891* (Halifax 1890)
34 Karl Baedeker, *The Dominion of Canada* ... (Leipzig 1907), 3rd ed., 51; RBB Papers, vol. 876, Diary, 1890.
35 DUA, *Dalhousie Gazette*, 26 November 1890 (vol. XXIII, no. 3); 17 December 1891 (vol. XXIV, no. 4); RBB Papers, vol. 876, Diary, 1891
36 See John Willis, *A History of Dalhousie Law School* (Toronto 1979), 9.
37 Halifax *Evening Mail*, 7 February 1891, probably copied from the *Morning Herald* of the same day
38 RBB Papers, vol. 876, 544147
39 NAC, Harold Daly Papers, R.B. Graham to H.M. Daly, 28 January 1948, from Winnipeg. This letter was brought to my attention by Professor John English, University of Waterloo, to whom I am most grateful. Graham graduated from Dalhousie Law School in 1893, the same year as R.B. Bennett. RBB's marks may also have been partly due to work as assistant librarian, and to his being premier of the mock parliament and then leader of the opposition.
40 RBB Papers, vol. 876, 544432, Diary, 14 November 1890; 544311, Diary (25 May 1891; 544313 (7 June 1891); 544315 (14 June 1891)
41 Ibid., vol. 875, 543794, Alma Russell to Alice Millar, 12 November

1948. Alma Russell destroyed many of her early letters from Bennett, but a few later ones, from 1914 onward, have turned up in the New Brunswick Museum in Saint John, under title of Alma Russell Papers.

42 DUA, *Dalhousie Gazette*, 17 October 1892 (vol. XXV, no. 1); 25 November 1892 (vol. XXV, no. 3); DUA, MS-1-13, Faculty of Law, Box 1, Record of the Dalhousie Mock Parliament, 1888–1900

43 NAC, Harold Daly Papers, Graham to Daly, 28 January 1948

44 House of Lords Record Office, Lord Beaverbrook Papers, vol. 66, Max Aitken to RBB, 29 December 1896, from Chatham

45 *Chatham World*, 3 June 1896; V.A. Danville's recollections, in RBB Papers, vol. 875, 543813

46 Ibid., 544086, Miller Salter to RBB, 29 December 1896, from Chatham

47 Ibid., vol. 876, 544077, James Lougheed to RBB, 26 December 1895, from Calgary

48 Beaverbrook, *Friends*, 12; Ernest Watkins, *R.B. Bennett*, 30

49 *Chatham World*, 13 January 1897, reporting dinner of 9 January

50 Beaverbrook Papers, vol. 66, Max Aitken to RBB, 23 December 1896. Max added, 'This ink is frozen, this pen is bad, and this office is cold.'

51 Slightly misquoted from Bishop Berkeley's 'On the Prospect of Planting Arts and Learning in America,' c. 1730. The original has 'world,' not 'star.'

52 *Chatham World*, 13 January 1897

53 RBB Papers, vol. 875, 543747–8. This is an article by Fred Griffin for the *Toronto Star Weekly* in November 1938, which went through drafts under Alice Millar and RBB.

54 Ibid., vol. 874, 543717, Brig.-Gen. J.S. Stewart to A.E. Millar, 27 September 1947, from Lethbridge, recalling a 1934 conversation with RBB.

2 WORK, RICHES, AND EMPIRE

1 Karl Baedeker, *The Dominion of Canada ...* (Leipzig 1907) 3rd ed., 256

2 Calgary *Daily Herald*, 3 January 1939, reporting interview with RBB

3 Grant MacEwan, *Eye-Opener Bob* (Edmonton 1957), 21, quoting the Wetaskiwin *Free Lance*, 23 October 1902

4 RBB Papers, vol. 877, 545817 RBB to Mrs. William Warren of Carstairs, 1 May 1903

5 From an article in 1938 prepared by Fred Griffin of the *Toronto Star Weekly*, with the help of Alice Millar and RBB. RBB Papers, vol. 875, 543740 *et seq.*

6 Ibid., 877, 544883, RBB to H.H. Stewart, Hopewell Hill, 7 May 1903, noting that the principalships of Calgary high school and the public school were vacant

7 Ibid., 545767, RBB to R.W. Harrington, Nelson, BC, March 1903, from Calgary

8 Ibid., 545790, RBB to Shannon Bowlby, Berlin, Ontario, 8 April 1903

9 Ibid., 544727, RBB to C.H. Parker, Nanaimo, 5 March 1903

10 Ibid., vol. 876, 545787, RBB to Rev. Wm. Briggs, Toronto, 7 April 1903

11 House of Lords Record Office, Beaverbrook Papers, vol. 66, Wm. Aitken to RBB, 6 December 1897, from Newcastle

12 Lord Beaverbrook, *Friends: Sixty Years of Intimate Personal Relations with Richard Bedford Bennett* (London 1959), 18

13 Ibid., 19

14 Lord Beaverbrook, *Courage: The Story of Sir James Dunn* (Fredericton 1961), 56

15 RBB Papers, vol. 875, 543935, 543948

16 Ibid., vol. 877, 544737, RBB to Borden, 10 March 1903, private

17 See C.C. Lingard, *Territorial Government in Canada: The Autonomy Issue in the Old North-West Territories* (Toronto 1946), 107.

18 RBB Papers, vol. 877, 544828, RBB to Borden, 30 March 1903, personal

19 Robert Craig Brown, *Robert Laird Borden: a Biography*, vol. I, 1854–1914 (Toronto 1975), 53; RBB Papers, vol. 877, 544876, RBB to Borden, 4 May 1903

20 Ibid., 544913, RBB to Borden, 3 June 1903

21 Ibid., 545321, RBB to Borden, 29 August 1904

22 Ibid.; see also Brown, *Borden*, 75–6

23 Sara Jeannette Duncan, *The Imperialist* (1904), edited and with an

introduction by Claude Bissell (Toronto 1961), 230, 232

24 Willoughby Maycock, *With Mr. Chamberlain in the United States and Canada, 1887–88* (Toronto 1914), 105

25 RBB Papers, vol. 899, 562698

26 Beaverbrook, *Friends*, 25; Beaverbrook Papers, vol. 66, RBB to Max Aitken, 21 December 1903, from Montreal, and 23 December 1903, from Saint John.

27 Canada, House of Commons, *Debates 1912–13*, cols. 3942–62 (25 February 1913)

28 Ibid., cols. 3995–6

29 Ibid., col. 3998

30 Beaverbrook Papers, vol. 66, Bennett's address of 9 May 1947 to British Internal Combustion Engine Manufacturers Association

31 Ibid., RBB to Max Aitken, 17 February 1914, from Calgary

32 Beaverbrook *Friends*, 54–64

33 A.J.P. Taylor, *Beaverbrook* (New York 1972), 244

34 Calgary *Daily Herald*, 7, 8, 9, 17 July 1902

35 RBB Papers, vol. 875, 543838, Robert Rogers's interview with Dr G.D. Stanley, *c.* 1948–9; James H. Gray, *R.B. Bennett: The Calgary Years* (Toronto 1991), 102–3

36 Beaverbrook Papers, vol. 66, RBB to Max Aitken, 9 December 1911, from Ottawa

37 Canada, House of Commons, *Debates 1914*, cols. 3734–8 (14 May 1914)

38 See L.A. Knafla, 'Richard "Bonfire" Bennett: The Legal Practice of a Prairie Corporation Lawyer, 1898–1913' in Carol Wilton, ed., *Beyond the Law: Lawyers and Business in Canada, 1830 to 1930* (Toronto 1990), 363, 376. Bennett would have much disliked being comprehended under such a title as that of the book. James Gray, in his biography of Bennett's early years, has an account of this incident on pp. 199–202.

39 Canada, House of Commons, *Debates 1911–12*, cols. 17–18 (20 November 1911)

40 Ibid., col. 25

41 Ibid., col. 26

42 Ibid., *Debates 1927*, 1777–8 (16 March 1927); also *Debates 1926*, pp. (1974–5) quoting Neville Chamberlain, 22 September 1925

43 Taylor, *Beaverbrook*, 14
44 Beaverbrook Papers, vol. 66, Max Aitken to RBB, 18 November 1909; RBB to Max Aitken, 12 December 1909
45 Ibid., RBB to Max Aitken, 31 January 1910, personal and confidential
46 Ibid., Max Aitken to RBB, 20 June 1911; ibid., vol. G1 Box 2, Max Aitken to J.L. Stewart (editor of the *Chatham World*), 5 December 1911, from London
47 Ibid., vol. 66, RBB to Max Aitken, 18 May 1911, from Calgary
48 Ibid., RBB to Max Aitken, 9 December 1911 from Ottawa
49 RBB Papers, vol. 875, 543839, Dr G.D. Stanley's reminiscences, as given to Robert Rogers, 1948–9
50 Ibid., 543846–7, John Brownlee's reminiscences
51 *Calgary City Directories*, 1908–24, trace this history.
52 MacEwan, *Eye-Opener Bob*, 93–4
53 RBB Papers, vol. 875, 543745, Fred Griffin draft of interview with RBB and Alice Millar, sent to Alice Millar, 28 November 1938, from the *Toronto Star Weekly*
54 This story appeared after Bennett's death, in Regina *Leader-Post*, 5 July 1947.
55 Calgary *Daily Herald*, 25 October 1927, reporting interview with RBB

3 MILDRED BENNETT, HAZEL COLVILLE, AND THE WAGES OF POWER AND EXILE

1 See James H. Gray, *R.B. Bennett: The Calgary Years* (Toronto 1991), 276.
2 New Brunswick Museum, Alma Russell Papers, RBB to Alma Russell, Thanksgiving Day, 1927 (7 November); RBB to Max Aitken, 10 November 1927, quoted in Lord Beaverbrook, *Friends: Sixty Years of Intimate Personal Relations with Richard Bedford Bennett* (London 1959), 49
3 *Winnipeg Tribune*, 12 October 1927; *Saturday Night* (Toronto), 22 October 1927
4 RBB Papers, vol. 899, 562800, RBB to R.P. Bowles, 23 October 1928,

personal. Bowles was soliciting a contribution to Mount Allison University, and Bennett replied that he could not support Mount Allison, Calgary, and Alberta charities as well as the Conservative party, to say nothing of the claims of his own university (Dalhousie).

5 Canada, Senate, *Debates* 563 *et seq.* (1 July 1947). See also RBB Papers, vol. 1005.

6 Rod Finlayson, 'That Man Bennett,' 45. This manuscript is in the Finlayson-Wilbur Correspondence, NAC, MG31, D19. It was completed by Finlayson, with Wilbur's help, in 1966, but remains unpublished. My copy comes from J.R.H. Wilbur, part of a consignment of Wilbur papers and notes on RBB, for which I am most grateful to Dr Wilbur.

7 Ibid., 44

8 Ibid., 63

9 Ibid., 454

10 Ibid., 2. A few words about Bennett's secretaries is apropos. Arthur Merriam was a government official, paid as secretary to the president of the Privy Council. Rod Finlayson was hired by Bennett late in 1931 to act as political private secretary and troubleshooter. He was paid $300 a month by the government and an additional $200 out of Bennett's own pocket. Alice Millar was technically assistant private secretary, who had been with him in Calgary since 1914, and who would remain with him all his life. She was assisted in the office by Muriel Black and her sister Mildred There was also Mlle Adele Dupuis who did letters in French. There is a full description of this operation by RBB in a letter to Manion in 1938, when Manion was taking over as leader of the opposition. See NAC, Robert Manion Papers, vol. 4, RBB to Manion, 12 July 1938.

11 Finlayson, ms., 46–7

12 Beaverbrook Papers, G/19, Alice Millar to Beaverbrook, 14 June 1957, from Vancouver: interview, Miss Muriel Black, 7 January 1989, Ottawa; Finlayson ms., 300

13 Beaverbrook Papers, G/19, Alice Millar to Beaverbrook, 14 June 1957; RBB Papers, vol. 899, 562968, RBB to Bishop Felix Couturier, 22 March 1933, personal

14 Beaverbrook Papers, G/19, Alice Millar to Beaverbrook, 14 June 1957

15 RBB Papers, vol. 355, 237221, RBB to Earl of Bessborough, 21 November 1933, enclosing twelve pages of recommendations for honours; ibid., 237190, Secretary of State for Dominion Affairs to RBB, 19 December 1933, telegram, secret, cypher, personal. See also the Ottawa *Morning Journal*, 11 January 1934.

16 Beaverbrook Papers, vol. 66, Red Cooper to Beaverbrook, 24 September 1947, from Paradise Camp, Lake Louise

17 *Winnipeg Free Press*, 9 July 1938, article by J.B. McGeachy; R.J. Manion, *Life Is an Adventure* (Toronto 1936), 293–4

18 *Pembroke Bulletin*, 21 March 1938, quoting Agnes Macphail's home-town paper, probably the *Owen Sound Comet*. The reporter is quoting her own words.

19 RBB Papers, vol. 899, 562949, Mrs Doris Gillis to RBB, 25 January 1933; for Bennett's relations with Charlotte Whitton, see P.T. Rooke and R.L. Schnell, *No Bleeding Heart: Charlotte Whitton, a Feminist on the Right* (Vancouver 1987), 85–7, 105–6; see also James Struthers, *No Fault of Their Own: Unemployment and the Canadian Welfare State 1914–41* (Toronto 1983), 77–9.

20 New Brunswick Museum, Alma Russell Papers, RBB to Alma Russell, Sunday, n.d. (The envelope is postmarked 1 November 1914, a Sunday.)

21 Beaverbrook Papers, vol. 66, Bennett to Max Aitken, 24 July 1904. (The date is taken from the postmark on the envelope.)

22 Beaverbrook, *Friends*, 84. This is a revised version of articles by Lord Beaverbrook that first appeared in *Weekend Magazine* in 1959; RBB Papers, vol. 895, RBB to his brother Ronald, 5 March 1940. This concerned Ronald's son, also called Ronald, who wanted to be married. It shocked Bennett, for Ronald had no profession and no savings.

23 NAC, MG28, IV-2, Progressive Conservative Party Records, Bennett file

24 These reports cover only the period after 1935, however. See RBB Papers, vol. 899, 554997 to 555124.

25 Ibid., vol. 875; 543943, Mrs R.P. Allen to Alice Millar, 18 May 1948, from Fredericton; ibid., 543795, Alma Russell to Alice Millar,

12 November 1948, from Victoria
26 Ibid., 544067, Mildred to RBB, n.d., March 1897
27 Ottawa *Evening Citizen*, 2 April 1931; also in RBB Papers, vol. 897, 563025
28 Ernest Watkins, *R.B. Bennett* (Toronto 1963), 108. Watkins's book has one important virtue: he had the confidence of and conversations with Alice Millar available to him.
29 Rod Finlayson ms., 63
30 RBB Papers, vol. 899, Mildred to RBB, 18 August [1937], from Mayfair House, New York
31 See James H. Gray, *R.B. Bennett: The Calgary Years* (Toronto 1991), 232–8.
32 Beaverbrook Papers, G 20, Peter Howard's essay on relations between Beaverbrook and RBB, 14; *Lethbridge Herald*, 12 February 1946
33 RBB Papers, vol. 896, 561350, J.D. Matheson to RBB, 3 April 1931, from Calgary
34 Ibid., 561352, Peter McGibbon to RBB, 6 April 1931, from Bracebridge, Ontario; ibid., 561412, Rosa Rosenberg to RBB, 27 April 1931
35 Ibid., 561420, Mildred to RBB, n.d.
36 Ibid., Frank Regan to RBB, 15 April 1931, personal; S.J. Gauthier to RBB, 16 April 1931, from Montreal; RBB to Gauthier, 20 April 1931
37 Interview, Frances Stephens Ballantyne, Oakville, Ontario, 5 July 1989. I am most grateful to Mrs Ballantyne, Hazel Colville's daughter, for taking the trouble to see me and answer questions.
38 *Montreal Gazette*, 14 May 1931, has an obituary.
39 RBB Papers, vol. 946, 597767–72, 'The Manoir de Repentigny'
40 Ibid., 597742, Hazel Colville to RBB, 6 January 1930, from 1371 Pine Avenue, Montreal, her home. This first letter was however addressed 'My dear Mr. Bennett.'
41 McCord Museum Archives, McGill University, Hazel Colville Papers, RBB to Hazel Colville, Saturday [27 August 1932]. This letter, like many of RBB's handwritten ones, is not dated, only with the day of the week. The date is taken from the postmark on the envelope. RBB's handwriting is not always legible. His punctuation is idiosyncratic, too; he often liked to end sentences with a colon. In

the quotations that follow I have used RBB's system. These and other letters have been brought to my attention by Professor Carman Miller, Department of History, McGill University. I am most grateful to him.

42 The reference to Hazel Colville's step-mother is to Sir Edward Kemp's second wife, Mrs Norman Copping, whom he married in 1925. He died in 1929.

43 This may refer to the Imperial Conference of 1932.

44 Hazel Colville Papers, RBB to Hazel Colville, Sunday night, 9:30, approaching Fort William [29 August 1932]

45 Ibid., Tuesday, 20 September 1932, from Chateau Laurier

46 Ibid., Sunday, 25 September 1932, from Ottawa; Monday, 10 October 1932, from House of Commons

47 Ibid., Monday, 17 October 1932, from Toronto

48 Ibid., Monday, 31 October 1932, from Ottawa. The letter from Hazel Colville that RBB refers to is, sadly, missing, along with all the other letters from her.

49 Ibid., Tuesday, 1 November 1932, marked 'All Saints' Day'

50 Frances Stephens Ballantyne's recollection; interview, 5 July 1989

51 RBB Papers, vol. 946, 597744, RBB to editor, Boston Advertiser, 21 October 1932; ibid., 597745/9, J.W. Reardon to RBB, 22 October 1932, and 24 October 1932. The headline RBB objected to was 'Premier Bennett to marry wealthy widow is report.'

52 Hazel Colville Papers, RBB to Hazel Colville, Tuesday, 8 November 1932

53 Interview, Frances Ballantyne, 5 July 1989, Oakville, Ontario

54 Ottawa Evening Journal, 6 December 1932

55 Hazel Colville Papers, RBB to Hazel, 17 July 1933, from London

56 Ibid., RBB to Hazel, Friday night [28 July 1932]

57 Ibid., RBB to Hazel, Saturday night [23 December 1933]

58 Frances Stephens Ballantyne's recollection; interview, 5 July 1989

59 Hazel Colville went abroad and lived in Italy until 1937. She subsequently bought a house in Nassau, in the Bahamas, and used to play bridge with the Duke of Windsor when he was governor there. The Duchess's talents did not include bridge! Mrs Colville's health began to fail in the 1950s and she died on 26 October 1961, at the age of seventy-two.

60 Hazel Colville Papers. This is the first of three sonnets, 'Field of Honour' by Sara Henderson Hay, attached to RBB's letter of 20 September 1932.

61 *Toronto Daily Star*, 31 January 1933. For the general attitude of the *Star* to R.B., see Ross Harkness, *J.E. Atkinson of the Star* (Toronto 1963), 259–61.

62 RBB Papers, vol. 945, 597317, RBB to Borden, 5 October 1933, personal

63 Finlayson ms., 252

64 *In Regulation and Control of Aeronautics in Canada* (1932) AC 54. Lord Macmillan was one of the four other law lords who supported Lord Sankey's judgment.

65 Canada, House of Commons, *Debates, 1933* cols 4151, 4168 (21 April 1933); see also Frank W. Peers, *The Politics of Canadian Broadcasting, 1920–1951* (Toronto 1969), 101–21.

66 RBB Papers, vol. 954, 603751–2, Stanley to George Robinson, 7 August 1947, from Calgary; Robert B. Bryce, *Maturing in Hard Times: Canada's Department of Finance through the Great Depression* (Kingston and Montreal 1986), 135–9; Douglas Fullerton, *Graham Towers and His Times* (Toronto 1986), 47–54; RBB Papers, vol. 875, 543643, Finlayson, 'This Man Bennett,' 10. This last appears to be an early draft of the Finlayson ms. that contains some information not in the later and longer version. There are, furthermore, seven tapes of discussions between Finlayson and Dr. J.R.H. Wilbur, which are at the Glenbow Foundation, Calgary, RCT 726/1 to RCT 726/7. Tape 6 has relevant information.

67 Finlayson ms., 305

68 See James Gray, *Men against the Desert* (Saskatoon 1978), xi.

69 Glenbow Foundation, Finlayson Tapes, RCT 726/5

70 RBB Papers, vol. 889, 554997–5004 are medical bulletins in Canada, including a report of Dr J.C. Meakins of the Royal Victoria Hospital, Montreal, who went over the electro-cardiograms and diagnosed 'paroxysmal auricular fibrillation.' He said, 'I am afraid the situation looks serious and should be handled firmly for the time being at least.' Report of 12 March 1935. The English reports, 555005–6, confirm the Canadian diagnosis.

71 Beaverbrook Papers, vol. 66, Mildred to Beaverbrook, 8 September

[1935] from St Andrews, NB; Ernest Watkins, *Bennett*, 227

72 The figures are from J.M. Beck, *Pendulum of Power* (Toronto 1968), 220–1.

73 Watkins, *Bennett*, 231–3

74 RBB Papers, vol. 899, Mildred to RBB, 18 August [1937] from Mayfair House, New York; ibid., vol. 896, Mildred to RBB, n.d. [1938?]

75 RBB Papers, vol. 896, 561600, Meighen to RBB, 11 May 1938, from the Senate; ibid., 561651, O.D. Skelton to RBB, 12 May 1938; ibid., 561689, Alan Lascelles to RBB, 13 May 1938, from Buckingham Palace

76 Beaverbrook, *Friends*, 88–9

77 RBB Papers, vol. 875, 543740, Alice Millar answering Fred Griffin's questions for a November 1939 *Toronto Star Weekly* article

78 Glenbow Foundation, Finlayson Tapes, Tape 3, conversation reported by John Stevenson

79 Beaverbrook, *Friends*, 118–19

80 I owe this wonderful recollection, of course, to Jeffrey Simpson, in Halifax in 1987 doing research for his 1988 book on patronage, *Spoils of Power*.

81 Toronto *Saturday Night*, 12 March 1938, ' "R.B." says farewell'

Index

THE JOANNE GOODMAN LECTURES

1976
C.P. Stacey, *Mackenzie King and the Atlantic Triangle* (Toronto: Macmillan of Canada/Maclean Hunter Press 1976)

1977
Robin W. Winks, *The Relevance of Canadian History: U.S. and Imperial Perspectives* (Toronto: Macmillan 1979)

1978
Robert Rhodes James, 'Britain in Transition'

1979
Charles Ritchie, 'Diplomacy: The Changing Scene'

1980
Kenneth A. Lockridge, *Settlement and Unsettlement in Early America: The Crisis of Political Legitimacy before the Revolution* (New York: Cambridge University Press 1981)

1981
Geoffrey Best, *Honour among Men and Nations: Transformations of an Idea* (Toronto: University of Toronto Press 1982)

1982
Carl Berger, *Science, God, and Nature in Victorian Canada* (Toronto: University of Toronto Press 1983)

1983
Alistair Horne, *The French Army and Politics, 1870–1970* (London: Macmillan 1984)

1984
William Freehling, 'Crisis United States Style: A Comparison of the American Revolutionary and Civil Wars'

1985
Desmond Morton, *Winning the Second Battle: Canadian Veterans and the Return to Civilian Life, 1915–1930* (published with Glenn Wright as joint author, Toronto: University of Toronto Press 1987)

1986
J.R. Lander, *The Limitations of the English Monarchy in the Later Middle Ages* (Toronto: University of Toronto Press 1989)

1987
Elizabeth Fox-Genovese, 'The Female Self in the Age of Bourgeois Individualism'

1988
J.L. Granatstein, *How Britain's Weakness Forced Canada into the Arms of the United States* (Toronto: University of Toronto Press 1989)

1989
Rosalind Mitchison, *Coping with Destitution: Poverty and Relief in Western Europe* (Toronto: University of Toronto Press 1991)

1990
Jill Kerr Conway, 'The Woman Citizen: Transatlantic Variations on a Nineteenth-Century Feminist Theme'

1991
P.B. Waite, *The Loner: Three Sketches of the Personal Life and Ideas of R.B. Bennett, 1870–1947* (Toronto: University of Toronto Press 1992)